PRAISE FOR *STRIVING FOR JUSTICE*

❝ Nat Glover's Striving for Justice is the engrossing story of a young Black man who rose from the then-segregated city of Jacksonville, Florida to become one of the nation's most respected law enforcement professionals. I saw the impressive work Nat Glover did as an inspiring leader in his community, and his moving and important book is a powerful testament to one man's commitment to justice, crossing racial divides, and making the world a better place."

—President Bill Clinton, 42nd President of the United States, 1993–2001, Author of *My Life* and numerous other titles

❝ In *Striving for Justice* Nat Glover takes readers on his lifelong journey. We vividly see both where he came from and where we as a nation came from. He forces us to consider the often-troubling relationship we currently have between law enforcement and people of color and the fragile relationship between government and citizens. Glover's book is thoughtful, provocative, and a fascinating view of race, law, and society through one man's eyes and his journey through life."

—Justin Brooks, Director, California Innocence Project, California Western School of Law, Author of *You Might Go to Prison, Even Though You're Innocent*

❝ Like so many of our nation's true patriots, Nathaniel Glover's unwavering commitment to public service was grounded in his struggles and triumphs while growing up in a segregated community. As you read his memoir, *Striving for Justice*, and learn about his amazing rise to becoming one of our nation's most respected and effective sheriffs, you will quickly realize that courage, true grit, and determination were at the center of it all.

"Sheriff Glover knows firsthand that America's greatness is not the product of fear or inaction, but the result of one's willingness to boldly go above and beyond the call of duty.

"As a native of Jacksonville, Florida, and a veteran law enforcement officer who served as Orlando's 36th chief of police, I was blessed to have Sheriff Glover as a mentor, and I am proud to endorse this magnificent work. From his chilling account of Ax Handle Saturday to the day Sheriff Nathaniel Glover stepped up to meet the challenges of keeping his community safe while treating people with dignity, I am grateful Sheriff Glover chose to share his powerful story.

"When we know better, we are supposed to do better, and I believe that each person who reads his story, including those in the law enforcement community, will be inspired to accept nothing less than the best of who we are, and, more importantly, the best of what we can accomplish when we all Strive for Justice."

—Val Demings, former US Representative of Florida s 10th Congressional District and former Chief of the Orlando Police Department

Rarely do you come across someone who impacts your life in a way that can only be described as divine. Nat Glover is that kind of man. After surviving insurmountable odds, Nat didn't surrender to justifiable excuses. He decided to persevere with love, demonstrating that a person can be compassionate and forgiving even in the face of adversity.

"Nat has dedicated his life to finding ways to help others see and believe in their potential and to trust that the impossible can be possible. His memoir underlines the redeeming value for anyone to realize that while the challenges they see in front of them may seem larger than life itself, trusting in God's plan will open their hearts to receiving and achieving what is divinely intended for them.

"Nat uses his experiences to paint a vivid picture of the obstacles he had to overcome and how instead of claiming defeat, they became the very situations that propelled him into becoming the first Black sheriff in Jacksonville, Florida, and the first Black sheriff in the state of Florida in over a hundred years. His tenacity, compassion, collaboration, and desire to succeed forged a leadership style that garnered both great support and great opposition, the inevitable reality in law enforcement.

"This memoir is a must-read for law enforcement professionals, particularly those in any leadership capacity. Using our strength, knowledge, experience, and expertise, along with Nat's wisdom, can catapult lasting and effective change within and beyond our sphere of influence."

—Steve Casey, Executive Director,
Florida Sheriffs Association

I first met the legendary Nathaniel Glover in the late 1980s at the annual National Preventing Crime in the Black Community Conference. At the time, I was an Orlando police sergeant and I remember the buzz when both division chiefs Glover and Jerome Spates made appearances. I saw them as role models and remember conversations about their rise in rank.

"I celebrated when I heard the news about Nat Glover's election as the first Black Florida sheriff in 1995. His rise was inspirational to me and served as a catalyst for my own rise in rank as a law enforcement executive and politician. I was appointed as the first Black police chief in Orlando in 1998 and one of the first persons whom I called for advice was Sheriff Glover. In 2008, I was also elected the first Black sheriff in Orange County, Florida, only the third in Florida. I owe a debt of gratitude to Nat for the sage advice he gave me.

"I credit Nat Glover with encouraging me to run for mayor. He offered feedback on pitfalls to avoid based on his own experience. I am completing my fourth year as the fifth elected Orange County mayor, and I am presently seeking reelection. Given the tone of the times in which we are living, I agree with Nat that there is no better time for police reform than now! However, I must say that during my nearly four decades as a law enforcement officer, there were calls for police reform during the entire period. In other words, present-day calls for police reform are nothing new. America remains an imperfect nation but as we strive for perfection, America will change when we focus on our similarities as an ethnically diverse nation, rather than when we focus on our differences.

—Mayor Jerry L. Demings was sworn in on December
4, 2018, as the fifth elected mayor of Orange County and
is the first African American to serve in the role. He is
married to former US Representative Val Demings.

" The Nathaniel Glover story is the story of America, the best and worst aspects of life as a Black man in America. This emotional autobiography is a masterpiece of storytelling that takes its reader on an emotional journey that leads to the pinnacle of law enforcement and a celebrated life and career. The early setbacks in the life of Nathaniel Glover set the stage for a major comeback on a grand level in spite of trials and tribulations that would have stopped an average man dead in his tracks. Every chapter peels back a layer of agony, pain, and triumphs. Nathaniel shares his story without even an ounce of resentment or bitterness, the sign of an extraordinary spirit and a remarkable human being who never gave up on himself or his dreams."

—Alvin Brown, Mayor of Jacksonville, Florida (2011–2015)

STRIVING FOR JUSTICE

STRIVING FOR JUSTICE

A BLACK SHERIFF IN THE DEEP SOUTH

To Scott
Thank you for your dedication
to Goodwill and your service
to our community.

NATHANIEL GLOVER

Nat Glover

FREDERICK
DOUGLASS
BOOKS

Published by Frederick Douglass Books, an imprint of Forefront Books.

Distributed by Simon & Schuster.

Library of Congress Control Number: 2023907085

Print ISBN: 978-1637631775
E-book ISBN: 978-1637631782

Cover Design by Bruce Gore, Gore Studio, Inc.
Interior Design by Bill Kersey, KerseyGraphics

TABLE OF CONTENTS

DEDICATION

Mama, Daddy, and Eugene.
Thank you, my angels in Heaven,
for always watching over me.

FOREWORD

By Kenneth B. Morris, Jr.
Publisher, Frederick Douglass Books

Frederick Douglass, often called "the father of the civil rights movement," was one of the most celebrated intellectuals of his time and the foremost leader of the abolitionist movement in nineteenth century America. Born into slavery in 1818 and self-emancipated in 1838, he would become a bestselling author, journalist, newspaper publisher, and suffragist and serve as an adviser to President Abraham Lincoln throughout the Civil War. Douglass is still revered today for his unparalleled oratory, stirring writings, and tireless fight against racial injustice. As his great-great-great-grandson, I am humbled and proud to announce that his descendants are continuing the Douglass literary legacy by publishing Nat Glover's *Striving for Justice* under the newly launched Frederick Douglass Books imprint of Forefront Books.

When we were considering the first book to publish in the new venture, I kept gravitating toward Nat's manuscript and his remarkable life story. I could not help but think that Frederick Douglass would find tremendous satisfaction in Nat being the first African American elected sheriff in Jacksonville, Florida, and the first Black sheriff in the state of Florida in over a hundred years in the post-reconstruction South since Douglass was a "first" in law enforcement. In 1877, President Rutherford B. Hayes nominated my great-ancestor as the U.S. Marshal for the District of Columbia. When the U.S. Senate confirmed his nomination, he became the first African American ever confirmed for a presidential appointment. So it is perhaps divine providence that Nat's memoir be our "first" publication.

My great-great-great-grandfather would have appreciated how Nat prioritized effective public speaking and communication in his law enforcement agenda. Frederick Douglass is admired as one of the greatest orators in American history. Like Douglass, Nat understands that words have power and that what you say is just as important as how you say it. Perhaps inspired by the Great Abolitionist, Nat prioritizes communication skills for his law enforcement colleagues, and he understands that great oratory can impart dignity and agency. Throughout Douglass's life, he used his extraordinary rhetorical skills to speak truth to power and fight against social injustice, and he advocated for human rights for all people.

More than these similarities to Frederick Douglass, what kept drawing me back to Nat's memoir is that his life's journey is intense and compelling. With clear and captivating prose Nat tells the story of being born into one of the deepest enclaves of segregation and institutional racism in the Old South. He experienced unimaginable racial violence, yet he decided at an early age that the love of his community and his commitment to the bedrock values of justice and fairness would lead him to a career in law enforcement.

It is fascinating to follow Nat along the path that eventually led him to ". . . the very top of a once-racist law enforcement agency, ultimately leading officers who decades earlier barely tolerated my presence." *Striving for Justice* is not only a gripping memoir, it's also a powerful call to Americans to have the courage and the perseverance to understand why so many Black and Brown people distrust law enforcement.

Nat does not avoid speaking hard truths about the profession to which he dedicated his life. With the moral authority and determination of a leader who has "walked the walk," he pulls no punches when challenging leaders in law enforcement to address those practices and dynamics that continue to sow mistrust and resentment today in marginalized communities. I cannot help but think that Frederick Douglass would have appreciated Nat's courage and readiness to speak truth to power: an enduring part of the legacies of Frederick Douglass and Nat Glover.

Frederick Douglass once wrote, "If there is no struggle, there is no progress." *Striving for Justice* is a fitting title for this book. The struggle for justice and equality continues today. I am confident that Nat's examples of heroism, determination, and action will inspire you to be change agents, just like Frederick Douglass, and carry freedom's torch forward.

PREFACE

**If your mind can conceive it,
you can achieve it.**

Morning descended on downtown Jacksonville, Florida, with temperatures simmering at eighty-three degrees by 11 a.m. and heading to an afternoon steam bath in the high nineties. Oppressive humidity, nary a passing cloud or breeze. A blistering, brutal, and ultimately notorious day in the Deep South. The date? August 27, 1960.

Tyrannical racial segregation still was being enforced in Jacksonville and throughout the South. But the thick summer air was beginning to stir with protest, challenge, and action. Young African American men and young African American women were demanding change.

These small groups of civil rights activists advocated and adhered to a policy of nonviolence. Their strategy was to peacefully demand a bus seat of their choice, a classroom with white peers, and a cup of coffee at a segregated lunch counter.

These things don't seem like much to us today, do they? A bus seat? A decent education? A cup of coffee? But they were important. For us, these were the most fundamental elements of momentum toward true equality.

Now, during the summer of 1960, the national media was paying attention. White supporters were joining the cause and sometimes the protests. Musicians and other artists were taking notice. Before long, the whole world was watching—and listening.

> *We shall overcome*
> *We shall overcome*
> *We shall overcome, some day*
> *Oh, deep in my heart*
> *I do believe*
> *We shall overcome, some day*
> *We'll walk hand in hand*
> *We'll walk hand in hand*
> *We'll walk hand in hand, some day*
> *Oh, deep in my heart*
> *I do believe*
> *We shall overcome, some day*

In the sweltering heat of a summer day in 1960, in the segregated Deep South city of Jacksonville, Florida, a small group of young Black men and women risked their lives for the cause of justice. They bravely sat in an intimate space with rabid racists whose hot breath and spittle coated the young people's necks. The indomitable protestors would return the next day to face the vitriol again. And again. And again.

But one day, the predictable pattern of segregationists shifted, bent on more violence.

One of the white segregationists drove a truck chock-full of baseball bats and axe handles into the town square in order to beat the nonviolent Black protestors—but not only them. This mob's terrorism was unleashed on every Black person—young or old, man or woman, adult or child—within their crazed reach. Innocent blood ran in the streets from the mob's indiscriminate attacks.

No Black person was safe.

There were myriad shouts, curses, and two-handed swings. The air was filled with the dull thuds of wood meeting flesh, and the pavement was laden with streams of blood.

About an hour after the onslaught, a seventeen-year-old Black boy left his dishwashing job at Morrison's Cafeteria, across from the park. Warned earlier by his white supervisor of the violence that was taking place outside, he chose to stay at work to complete his tasks. When he was ready to depart for home, he found himself the only Black person now on the street. While the protestors had been run off, the angry mob lingered in the area. The young man stood out like a sore thumb and was quickly surrounded by a group of indignant vigilantes.

The assailants' faces, twisted with the rage of social dominance under the perceived threat of extinction, taunted the young man.

"Hey, boy!" an angry voice commanded from the crowd.

"Hey, nigger!" Another voice followed with just as much ferocious hate.

"What you doin' here?"

And then the menacing blows began. Through the blows, the teenager pleaded to a white officer observing the violence nearby: "Please. Help me!" The officer didn't move. With a smirk, he looked the other way. The teenage boy was at the complete mercy of the mob and the indifference of the law.

The day became known to history as Ax Handle Saturday.

I was that young man.

My name is Nat Glover, and I was there.

⚖

That was six decades ago. Sixty years. Our situation has changed somewhat. Our ambitions have advanced somewhat. Our lives have improved somewhat. But not enough. Not enough. Not any of it. Not. Enough.

Today, sixty years later, Black Americans are being shot dead by police for driving while Black.

Today, sixty years later, Black Americans are being shot dead for walking while Black.

Today, sixty years later, Black Americans are being shot dead for jogging while Black.

And today, sixty years later, Black Americans are being shot dead by police even for sleeping while Black.

When it comes to character, I try to give everyone the benefit of the doubt. I believe people deserve that until they prove otherwise. Also, it just makes strategic sense. Even if someone has a poor reputation and a history of bad behavior, I might have to work with that person or their supporters at some point down the road.

But there are limits, so I will be particularly measured during these next few paragraphs.

While many of these abuses against Blacks and others of color took place, too many of our "leaders" in Washington, state capitals, and local governments—some of whose lives were stained by racist statements and actions—looked the other way. During their catastrophic tenures, they openly embraced white supremacy and the violence it triggered. In addition, they facilitated the disease-ridden deaths of hundreds of thousands of Americans, including a disproportionate number of African Americans and other minorities. They and their enablers worked overtime to intimidate minority voters and suppress their right to cast ballots.

When one of these people, Donald Trump, sought reelection as president in 2020, he failed. But he was supported by nearly 47 percent of American voters—exactly 74,216,154 of the people with whom other Black people and I live in this country.

I almost wrote "share" in that last sentence— ". . . the people with whom other Black people and I share this country." But that would be inaccurate.

To *share* is to have an equal part, to be given an opportunity to shine. I believe that shining is displaying and exhibiting one's distinct and impactful abilities. People should be hopeful and expect to be placed in positions where they will shine, and Black people do not have that yet. Not any of that. Not even close. Not now, when police brutality, explicit and implicit racism, and deeply embedded white privilege remain so evident and prevalent, and wrong. Nevertheless, I believe that I have something to share and that I have been placed in a position to shine and to help others reach the place where they will shine. After all, I rose to the very top of a once-racist law enforcement agency, ultimately leading officers who decades earlier barely tolerated my presence. That is why I wrote this book, despite initial misgivings.

For years, friends and associates have urged me to put to paper the challenges I have confronted, the experiences I have endured and enjoyed, the setbacks, and the triumphs. "You have overcome," they would say. "You have achieved. You have been lifted up by others. You have an obligation to do the same, to show the way, to give back."

To be honest, I believe I have done that throughout my life, the work I have done, and the examples I have striven to create. I did not and do not want to appear arrogant or to be seen as what we would call back in my childhood neighborhood a "chest thumper." But I want to do more. I want to talk to you, the reader, about the circumstances I endured—my failures and successes—so that you can learn from my life.

Put concisely, I want this book to have redeeming value for others and to serve as a road map for getting there. I think—I hope—that it does.

⚖

I was born into and grew up within what generously could be called an underprivileged environment, an area that many would call a ghetto. There were obstacles, to put it lightly. Not every path I've taken has pushed me in the right direction. I have made mistakes, plenty of them, but I learned and overcame my errors, often with the assistance of remarkable people.

One of the secrets of whatever success I may have achieved is that I don't mind failing. In fact, some of my failures have turned out to spark some of my greatest victories. Even when I lose, I walk with a sense of knowing that there's another path. My path has been tweaked and adjusted, and I'm continuing to head toward something else that's been divinely orchestrated.

In the end, it comes down to this: I have life experience, and I know deeply that I have the responsibility to share it with others. Especially if you are young and impressionable. Especially if you are galvanized by the newly emerging challenges confronting law enforcement and the people it serves. Especially if you are considering a life in any challenging endeavor. It is incumbent upon us to leave the world a better place than we found it.

INTRODUCTION

When you're the only anything, when you're the first something, you're under constant scrutiny.

It pains me to say this, but unfortunately, much of white America looks upon Black Americans as somehow both the instruments of violence and the unsympathetic, even deserving, victims of violence.

According to federal health statistics, homicide has been the fifth-leading cause of death (pre-COVID) among Black men of all ages. Homicide also has been the second-leading cause of death of Black women below the age of twenty and the fourth-leading cause of death of Black women between twenty to forty-four years old.

At the same time, even after all the publicity, protests, and promises, extreme racial disparities remain when it comes to fatal police shootings. When researchers from Yale University and the University of Pennsylvania looked at the nation's 4,653 fatal police shootings between 2015 and May 2020, they found that unarmed Black suspects were killed three times more often than unarmed white Americans. Among armed suspects, Black people were killed 2.6 times more often than whites.

Three times more likely to be killed by police. In the United States of America during the twenty-first century.

As a law enforcement officer, now retired, it also pains me to say this, but police and sheriffs' departments now are considered by much of Black America as threats equal to or even greater than the criminals and other bad actors law enforcement officers are supposed to be … policing.

The proliferation of video and other recording devices in the hands of most citizens, along with body cameras now worn by many officers, intensify the scrutiny now imposed on and shouldered by police officers.

I will summarize some solutions here and delve into detail later in this book, but first, let me address this question to my white American readers: What if "protect and serve" suddenly didn't apply to you anymore? How would you conduct your lives? Teach your children? What if the people charged with enforcing the law and keeping the peace didn't trust, believe, or value you? Imagine fearing for your life, your spouse's life, your son's (*especially* your son's) or daughter's life, or your grandchild's life every time they leave the house. And now, after the 2020 shooting death of twenty-six-year-old Breonna Taylor of Louisville, Kentucky, whom police officers fatally shot as she left her bed, we are fearing for our lives and their lives, home or away, every second of every day and night. Think about fearing that you or your loved one will be shot dead by police because you're assumed guilty, dangerous, or threatening—simply because of the color of your skin. This still is our Black reality in the United States. Every second of every day and every night. This is our reality—a reality that typical white Americans simply never must contend with.

After achieving my unlikely childhood dream of becoming a police officer and detective, after moving up the ranks of the typically Southern sheriff's department of Jacksonville, Florida, I was elected in 1995 to lead that department as sheriff. I was the elected Black sheriff of a city previously known as a hotbed of racism, the first elected Black sheriff in the Deep South state of Florida at least since the Reconstruction Era—and I served in that capacity for eight years. I had a clear path to winning reelection to a third term, unopposed, but I decided instead to seek office as the city's first Black mayor. There will be much more about this later, but for now, know that this was not easy. I had to suppress my anger in favor of calculation and strategy to achieve what I did.

When you're the only anything, when you're the first something, you're under constant scrutiny. Some are praying for your success; many others are hoping for, waiting for, or even working toward your failure. Nevertheless, I instituted a variety of reforms that served the citizens of that county and city and served the officers sworn to protect those citizens. Those reforms included,

- banning the infamous "choke hold";
- creating a crisis intervention training program to help officers deal with emotionally disturbed people;
- initiating a community policing concept,
- placing officers' names on their patrol cars;
- creating neighborhood substations,
- establishing citizen advisory councils;
- visibly and regularly walking through all fifty-one subsectors that included ninety-three police beats under my jurisdiction (walk-and-talk sessions affectionately called by others "fast-walk-chatter"); and
- leading teams of residents, inmates, and others on neighborhood cleanup missions to re-instill local pride.

When I won the job, someone created this sign: "New Sheriff in Town. Nat Glover." When I retired from the department eight years later, the *Florida Times-Union*—then perceived by many as no friend of Black residents—published an editorial headlined "A Job Well Done."

"Glover exhibited courage and leadership in redefining the department's role in the community," the newspaper editors wrote. "The community is better for the legacy and example Glover leaves for his successor ... [He] is likely to be remembered for years by many in the community."

So with that background understood, I hereby break with much of this nation's current corps of sheriffs and police chiefs. I tell them now—and I tell you now—that, for too long, too many of them have tolerated bad, violent, and otherwise unworthy officers.

We—they—need to reform their departments and, in fact, the entire criminal justice system, including prosecutors, judges, and the prison system. The entire system is infected with implicit bias.

Don't get me wrong. For the most part, these people and these entities have lived up to the motto of "protect and serve." The vast majority of police officers and others in the criminal justice system are honorable people who take their responsibilities seriously, often at great personal risk.

Many police and sheriffs' departments have been allowed to operate independently, even arrogantly, and without community oversight. Minority communities were and continue to remain more likely than other communities not to have significant or even *any* input into policing practices that are underway in their neighborhoods.

To be fair, it should be noted that some communities—both Black and white—have been perfectly willing, from time to time, to look the other way when officers mishandled situations or even abused their authority, just so long as the streets remained "calm."

None of that changes two facts—that African American communities repeatedly cry out for more equitable, more sensitive treatment by police departments and that some officers simply are unsuited for police work. Their personality issues range from being overly aggressive and downright oppressive to being overtly prejudiced and unapologetically racist.

I am convinced that a number of the most grotesque slayings and beatings of Black citizens, from Rodney King to George Floyd to Breonna Taylor to so many—too many—others, could have been avoided if sheriffs and police chiefs had been more willing to confront these officers and, when necessary, their unions, and to cull these people from their departments.

When I was an officer and when I was sheriff, I certainly was able to identify the bad actors, and I am certain that today's rank-and-file officers can do the same.

It must be done.

Racism remains a reality in this country and in too many police departments. It is endemic. It is systemic. It is murderous. It can, however, be pierced. It can be penetrated, though it takes enormous effort and persistence.

Please do not jump to conclusions. This book is not and will not be a racial screed. It will be informed by race, as it should be, but not with a monolithic, unambiguous point of view.

I am keenly aware that much has already changed for the better. Take Jacksonville, for instance. Not only was I twice elected sheriff and almost elected mayor of that city, but I paved the way for another Black man to win the mayoralty just eight years after I ran for the election.

In addition, even as I write these words, I just learned that two Black councilmen were elected to serve as president and vice president of the city council, the second and third most powerful positions in Jacksonville. This is the first time that people of color have held both posts simultaneously in this predominantly white city-county.

At about the same time, the school board voted in June 2021 to rename six Jacksonville schools that carried names associated with the Confederacy and those who had enslaved some of the ancestors of students who currently attended those schools.

The arc of history is long, but it bends toward justice, as Dr. Martin Luther King, Jr. said, and Jacksonville's citizens, both Black and white, are bending justice's way too.

$$\Delta\overline{\Delta}$$

Nuance is the name of the game here, as is individuality, and we can never forget that. Too often, Black Americans allow all white people to be considered as a whole, and that is wrong. There always have been white people who want to do the right thing and who look for opportunities to do so.

For example, remember that seventeen-year-old who was washing dishes at Morrison's Cafeteria? That youth who was me? Well, as I was walking home one night after work in 1960, I was stopped by two white police detectives.

One thing led to another, and I was arrested and charged with petty larceny for the crime of—are you ready?—having two cloth napkins in my back pocket. We often used these napkins from Morrison's as handkerchiefs, given the perspiration generated by our work in the steamy dish room of a Deep South restaurant, but let's not dwell for now on the merits of the case.

Were the cops racist? Possibly. Others thought so. Perhaps influenced by those people, I've always thought so as well. They could have given me a break, and I can't imagine them arresting a white teenager in such an incident. To be completely fair, though, I suppose one could make the case that they were just doing their jobs.

But here's the thing: after spending a traumatic night in jail, I was met in the courtroom by my white boss, who vouched for me, and by my father's white boss, who vouched for my family. We all appeared before a white judge, who dismissed the charge and told me, "I never want to see you down here again." Later, the entire episode played a major role, rather contradictorily when you think about it, in my becoming a police officer—after the direct, affirmative intervention of the city's white mayor.

So you see my point here. Getting arrested by two presumed racist white cops turned out to be a transformational experience for me largely due to the response of people—who also were white—who leveraged their influence to vouch for me. This situation ended up being for my good and for the good of my community.

I believe foundationally in the Golden Rule: we should treat others as we desire to be treated, regardless of the circumstances. As sheriff, my community approach to policing reflected this mantra: "If a young person is killed on the Black Northside of Jacksonville, mothers on the white Southside of Jacksonville also should weep." I expected my officers to respect all members of the community we served. My expectations constructed a set of leadership philosophies that evolved over time.

As sheriff, I knew it was my task to sow seeds of leadership throughout the Jacksonville Sheriff's Office (JSO), placing my officers in a position to shine, in turn fostering trust and loyalty throughout the command. By focusing on my officers' individual skill sets, I became confident that I could send any member of our team to complete a critical assignment, from the richest to the poorest neighborhoods.

Key to this was my insistence that every member of my leadership staff attends public speaking training sessions, despite their frequent resistance. I had received such training, and I knew it to be a crucial asset for anyone who needs to communicate effectively with the public and even with colleagues. If you can't articulate your position, you'll never convince anyone of anything. (I also allowed and encouraged young inmates in the correction system to take public speaking classes. I wanted to enhance their confidence and self-esteem.)

Becoming a clear, comfortable, informative public speaker was particularly instrumental in my ability to win over the white community during times of tense law enforcement crises, as well as during my political campaigns. Let's face it: history was not on my side, and I felt the need to go the extra mile to demonstrate my ability to do the job I sought to be entrusted in doing so fairly, justly, and effectively. When you hear whispers such as, "Do you really think those white people are going to turn all those guns over to you?" you know instinctively that public communications skills are going to come in handy.

Foundationally, I always have believed in reaching across the aisle, whether politically or religiously or demographically. The Jacksonville Sheriff's Office is now fully integrated. Not only that, but around 30 percent of the current (white) sheriff's command staff is African American. I mention this because it is important to highlight the progress that has been made, although there's still much to be done. More widely, no one in our community should have been surprised when I supported protections for the city's LGBTQ community as part of our closer attention to human rights for all. That expansion added sexual orientation, gender identity, and gender expression to the list of protected categories. This ensures or at least tries to ensure that no one endures discrimination in the workplace, in the housing market, or in public accommodations such as restrooms and locker rooms.

In fact, after being elected sheriff in 1995, one of my first official acts was to promote the first openly gay female officer to the department's command staff. Carol Hladki richly deserved the position as assistant chief and zone commander. Carol continued her rise through the ranks until she retired in 2016 as director of patrol and enforcement, the number-three position in the entire department.

Often during community gatherings, I'm asked to sit at the head table and deliver the opening prayer. I'm always humbled by these requests, which come from individuals of virtually all faiths and denominations. At the end of my life, when people ask, "Did Nat Glover make a difference in someone's life?" I would like someone to stand up and say, "Why, yes. Yes, he did."

And all of it began with a young boy's dream in a "shotgun" house at 734 Minnie Street in an all-Black neighborhood of northwest urban Jacksonville. A mother, a father, four sisters, and one brother. All of us crammed into two bedrooms. These were my people, and these were my formative years.

CHAPTER 1

EARLY LIFE AND FAMILY

I have not a moment to waste.

Everyone has a genesis story. Mine was forged by taking the hand I was dealt and making it work. It was forged in the crucible of the work ethic of my mother; the spirituality of my father; the pervasive feeling of poverty that doesn't quite leave; the tenacity of my brother, Eugene; the gift of community support; and the grumbling of discrimination. Yet I firmly believe divine intervention was the main force at hand throughout my life's story.

Throughout my life, many people have seen things in me that I do not always see in myself: determination, wisdom, and trustworthiness, among other qualities. I enjoy mentoring because, so many times, I see similarities between my experiences and that of my mentees—and I can coach them out of making the same mistakes I did.

All of this starts, as it does in one way or another for everyone, with parents and parenting. My parents were Arsie Glover, born in Ocilla, Georgia, on June 28, 1918, and Nathaniel Glover Sr., born in Walterboro, South Carolina, on October 15, 1912. Ocilla, incorporated only twenty-one years before my mother's birth, was little more than a secluded cotton-loading railroad stop of 1,100 residents. Walterboro, then a remote hamlet of 1,600 people, was known as the "Front Porch of South Carolina's Low Country."

In both cases, we're talking about the deepest of the Deep South. Black people suffered under conditions all too similar to enslavement— we were held hostage to the whims of white folks when it came to housing, education, employment, and quality of life. Nobody wants to live in an invisible prison. These were the places of my parents' origins and the sources of their expectations.

When she was able to find work, my mother generally performed domestic duties for white people. She also spent several years working in the housekeeping department of the now-defunct Duval Medical Center in Jacksonville. Even when she couldn't find regular work, she frequently served white former employers who brought clothing to our house for her to launder and iron. She had a tenacious work ethic. She went above and beyond the call of duty, taking on multiple tasks and completing them effectively and efficiently, never complaining, and always abiding in giving the same effort and energy at home. Her work ethic was so contagious that I caught it, and it has remained with me throughout my life.

This work ethic also was shared by my father, though in a quieter way. He was a plasterer and a finisher of pools. He sang in a spiritual quartet for many years and later became a minister of the gospel. He ultimately achieved the distinction and honor of being the pastor of his own church.

The six of us children—four girls and two boys—survived adolescence and beyond. In order of birth, we were Eugene, Bessie, me, Virginia,

Shirley, and Bertha. Eugene, Bessie, and Virginia have died, but I remain in close and constant contact with Bertha and Shirley, both of whom are married and blessed with children. Another sister, Patricia, died shortly after birth. I later learned, just before my father's death, that I had two other sisters, Gloria and Vanessa. These sisters were from my father's side.

My mother was a strict disciplinarian. Nothing she said ever was challenged by any of her children. She had, at best, a third- or fourth-grade education, and she was determined that we would advance in school much further than that.

One day it occurred to me that I was the only one in the neighborhood in my age group who was going to school every day. Still, I was overly influenced by three dropouts I hung out with. They seemed to have been doing very well—one always seemed to have a pocket full of money, one had a car, and one had a girlfriend. I didn't have any of those things.

I went to my mother with the brilliant idea of also quitting school. She found my plan less than brilliant. To be precise, she actually stopped me midsentence and said, "Let me help you with that. Son, if you're going to stay in this house, you're going to school. Period."

And so I did.

At that moment, I didn't think that she was the coolest mom. The coolest mothers, I thought, allowed their kids not to go to school. But I was so wrong, and she was so right.

To this day, I believe—no, I *know*—that my mom saved my life right there. Peer groups often are good for us, but sometimes they can sweep us in the wrong direction. If I had dropped out of school, I almost certainly would have ended up in prison or prematurely in the cemetery.

Like my father, Momma was a deeply spiritual and devout person, with values that she tucked into her children. She was a mother of mothers. She ingrained spiritual values into my siblings and me by demonstrating a life of compassion, faith, generosity, civility, trustworthiness, and honesty. Her words, actions, and deeds always aligned, never leaving us feeling like we didn't know exactly what she meant, felt, or expected.

Our father, who also had, at best, only an elementary school education, was not a strong disciplinarian. To the contrary, he generally tried to mitigate some of the punishments or sanctions imposed by our stern mother. Pardon the obvious remark from me (the former sheriff), but in this sense, my father and mother played the stereotypical roles of good cop / bad cop.

Daddy died on October 15, 1987; Momma passed on September 24, 2010. We miss them dearly and daily.

$$\text{⚖}$$

The house we rented, at 734 Minnie Street, stood between Beaver and Logan Streets. As I've said, this was an all-Black neighborhood, and it existed a bit uneasily about one mile northwest of downtown Jacksonville.

Now my former home is the site of a business development center and several social-benefit service agencies, which I find rather satisfying. Everything changes over time, not always for the best. But this—a building that serves my community and sits on the site of my childhood home—yes, I'll take that.

Generally speaking, however, the neighborhood, now somewhat cut off from downtown by the roaring, intertwined ribbons of Interstate 95, has fallen into disrepair. In order for any neighborhood to thrive, it needs intentional care, commerce, and access to community resources. The old neighborhood shows signs of neglect as a result of being intentionally cut off from these things. You can't choke an area and then be angry that it stops breathing.

Back in my day, Minnie Street was lined primarily by two types of houses. Two-story houses would shelter two families, one upstairs and one downstairs. The other type of residential building was called a "shotgun house." It was a single-family home divided into a tiny front porch, two bedrooms, a kitchen, a single bathroom, and a vest pocket back porch.

A shotgun house is where the Glover family lived. Two concrete steps atop the dirt. Creaking wooden floor. Walls that barely seemed to defy gravity. That was our house.

Why were these houses, here in Jacksonville and in many other places, called shotgun homes? Because, due to the design and room layout, a person could stand in front of the open front door, aim and fire a shotgun, and the pellets—theoretically, not actually, thank God—could fly straight through the place and out the open back door without touching anything. It was here that my mother, father, and younger sisters slept in the front room while I, along with my older brother and older sister, slept in the back room.

As renters who sometimes fell behind in our payments, we often were subjected to "inspections" by rental agency employees who rather threateningly took "inventory" of our possessions. This, of course, was the clearest possible signal that we better figure out how to catch up on the rent.

My parents were good providers when they could find work, but too often, work and money were scarce. Even so, they always figured it out, and we were never tattooed by the shame of eviction.

Poverty was an everyday experience, as natural as breathing or eating. It cut deeply into one's soul. We lived under the constant threat of home-lessness when there was more month at the end of the money. There were nights when candles provided the only light in the house. My father worked hard to provide for us, but there was always a looming concern that work would be scarce, resulting in smaller portions of food on our plates and recycled clothing shared among us children.

I recall many nights when the heat was stifling, and the air seemed too thick to breathe. Open windows and long hours sitting on our front porch were our desperate attempts to cool off. My parents were sure to keep us fed, and although family meals were not fancy feasts, our bellies were kept from growling. I understood that we were not as fortunate as others, but our lack became a life lesson for me that expresses itself to this day in deep gratitude for the financial and other blessings I have—and it expresses itself through devotion to charity. Among other things, I never drive past a panhandling street person without reaching into my pocket for five dollars or more—often much more. I regularly give worthy recipients a $20 bill. Once, I came across a woman in need of gas money. I hesitantly decided to give her a $50 bill. I hesitated because I thought she might have been running a scam. However, she eased my fears when she ran behind me to return the $50, assuming I'd made a "mistake." But it was no mistake at all. I intended to give her the $50. Her honesty led me to think about the Lord speaking to me, telling me that I should do what I'm supposed to do by helping others and not by worrying about their reaction because that's not my responsibility. And I have quietly, from behind the scenes, paid outstanding bills of as much as $1,500 to help a struggling business remain afloat.

I tell you this not to boast but to illustrate the persistent effects of childhood poverty and, in my opinion, the proper way to respond to it later in life. Nearly everyone in our neighborhood endured similar financial pressures and embarrassing experiences, but most seemed to make it from week to week. Alas, some were more, let's call it *enterprising*. They sold illegal whiskey from at least three illicit "moonshine houses" within two blocks of our home. On many occasions, I saw police officers going into those houses and coming out without taking any enforcement action. It was thought by many in the neighborhood that these officers were pocketing their regular payoff to look the other way. I can conjure no other explanation.

⚖

To understand me, you must understand my place—the sprawling city of Jacksonville. Long home to Native Americans; settled by Europeans in the mid-1500s; and later named for Andrew Jackson, one-time president and notorious evictor and slayer of Native Americans, Jacksonville sits on the north and south sides of the wide and lengthy St. Johns River. African Americans, nearly all of them enslaved to toil on nearby plantations, populated much of the area during the 1700s and 1800s. Once freed, many of them settled just west of Jacksonville in the town of LaVilla, a square-mile area that became a center of Black commerce and culture.

As Jacksonville grew, it absorbed LaVilla in 1887. Nevertheless, LaVilla remained predominantly Black, even as African Americans slowly expanded into other parts of the city, primarily along the river's north bank. Thus, Black Jacksonville and white Jacksonville, centered around a small downtown and along the southern bank, remained largely separate. Separate and not remotely equal.

For decades and deep into the twentieth century, even as the region emerged as a papermaking power and the city became known as a financial center, virtually every lever of power was grasped tightly and exclusively by white Jacksonville. Consequently, unemployment and blight increasingly shadowed LaVilla and other Black neighborhoods.

Change, slow and sometimes violent, did begin to arrive during the 1960s civil rights movement. It came despite the 1968 merger of largely Black Jacksonville with its surrounding, predominantly white Duval County. This created the nation's largest municipality at nine hundred square miles.

It also created an unusual case of nomenclature. The city's police force was combined with the county's law enforcement agency, oddly known as the Duval County Road Patrol. The new entity was and remains the

Jacksonville Sheriff's Office. It uses the name of Duval County's largest city, but due to consolidation, it serves and oversees the entire county.

Consolidation clearly was intended to dilute the voting power of Jacksonville's Black residents, and it did. One study found that the African American share of the dramatically enlarged city dropped from 41 percent before consolidation to 20 percent after consolidation.

Jacksonville's Black citizens had been promised that consolidation would produce resources sufficient to repair, improve, and modernize the creaky infrastructure of their neighborhoods. Still, all of that was very slow in coming.

As I was growing up, my neglected neighborhood stood adjacent to and effectively served as an extension of La Villa. By then, La Villa had long been just a largely neglected section of Jacksonville, but it had maintained its Black identity despite being starved of proper resources.

In fact, my first elementary school was not only in La Villa—it actually was named Old La Villa School. "Old" was the key word. Though my teachers tried their best, the building was primitive, constructed from wood, and our textbooks were tattered hand-me-downs. Our educators were largely required to fend for themselves. We all were required to fend for ourselves. The deficiency of resources and representation was the symptom of the disease—segregation.

I am fortunate to still be here to write this book. A certain measure of luck is present in all our lives, in the survival of each of us. But, in particular, in mid-twentieth century America, being Black and poor were not terrific leading indicators of a long life.

As a toddler, I contracted double pneumonia. The prognosis was grim. During those years, pneumonia was one of the top infectious causes of death in the United States. Thankfully, the toll has diminished as penicillin and other therapeutics were developed, but pneumonia remains a grave threat to survival worldwide and in the United States, even today. And the COVID-19 pandemic, which often produces lethal cases of pneumonia, has made things much worse once again.

Back in the mid-1940s, when I became ill, my mother brought me to the doctor. He was incredibly compassionate, but he was not encouraging. The few existing therapeutic options back then were not available for poor Black families. Cures were commodities—luxuries afforded to those with the financial means.

"Take him home and make him comfortable," the doctor told my mother. He did not explicitly say much more than that, but the implication was clear: I was not expected to survive. And yet here I am, nearly eighty years later, still happily married to Doris, the father of Michael and Clementine, the grandfather of three, and the great-grandfather of seven. My faith and strong belief in God have been the light that has guided my path to navigating the storms and calms of life with grace, humility, steadfastness, and perseverance. Consequently, in my adulthood, I have always sensed that I live my life on borrowed time. I have not a moment to waste.

I often outworked my peers. I came in early and stayed late. I embraced tasks others avoided. I volunteered to work holidays and double shifts. This impressed my supervisors and served as a key to my career growth and to my development as a leader. Unfortunately, all this took away time and experiences I could have been spending and sharing with my family (which I now strive to make up for). It felt like I had no choice. I had to meet my purpose. I had to achieve my divine destiny.

I mentioned that others frequently see in me something that I do not readily see myself. This phenomenon began around the time I developed my first lasting memories, and it involved my mother—the disciplinarian, the perfectionist. Many people assert the aspirational theme, "Anything worth doing is worth doing well." For my momma, this was not merely aspirational. It was an embedded way of life. She would often assign me tasks that required diligence, persistence, and a high level of thoroughness. Somehow, I seemed to earn more of her trust than my siblings. Though I was the middle child, with an older brother and an older sister, Momma consistently assigned me the lion's share of chores and responsibilities that required care and long-range attention.

Everyone in our household played with our dog—appropriately named Trouble—but I alone was responsible for ensuring that he was fed and had plenty of water. I took these responsibilities seriously. I imagine that, back then, I mostly wanted to please my mother and, of course, care for Trouble. But now I realize I also was cultivating my inner work ethic and sense of purpose. All of this seemingly impressed the people around me. "He wasn't the type to get into trouble," former neighbor Willie Mae DeLoach told a reporter for the (Fort Lauderdale) *Sun-Sentinel* after I was elected sheriff. "I knew he was going to make something of himself. I just didn't know what."

As we all aged, my parents continued to place exceptional responsibilities upon me, the middle child, rather than my older siblings. For instance, they appointed me as a cosigner on their checking account. After my father died, their other assets were placed in my name because Daddy knew that I would take care of Momma.

To this day, I apparently maintain a reputation of trustworthiness and loyalty. For some reason, people frequently tell me their secrets. I am flattered by this, though sometimes this knowledge is a burden.

During my youth, it wasn't just my parents and Miss DeLoach who identified something special in me, something worth enriching. One of our neighbors, a kind man we called Mr. Fred, worked as a railroad employee. Although the work was difficult and kept him away from home for major periods, it came with an attractive fringe benefit—free train rides across the country.

Back then, riding a train was analogous to today's cruise or international plane trip, and Mr. Fred and his wife, Miss Gertrude, who, by then, had grown children, enjoyed the opportunity to take a free trip every year.

This made them the envy of our largely impoverished and housebound community. And for several years, when I was in elementary school, they would walk across the street to our house and ask my mother if I could accompany them on one of their amazing trips to faraway places. Not my older brother or older sister. Not my younger sisters. *Me.*

I don't remember much about these trips. However, one thing that does stand out in my memory is that white people did what Mr. Fred told them to do; he was in charge. These trips changed me forever, and I was no longer just another Black boy living in another Black ghetto. On those trips, I felt special.

They say that travel is growth; it enlarges our lives and our experiences and our expectations. No one knows this better than I do. We didn't have many cultural opportunities when I was growing up. No live theater. Few resources to buy admission to movies. Admission cost only sixteen cents back then, but Momma allowed me to join my friends at the movies only once every two weeks. "Did you go last week?" she would respond to my request. "No? OK, you can go this week."

Television was not yet readily available. But we did have a tabletop radio that delivered untold hours of entertainment, much diversion, and, in my case, a deep and abiding ambition. I was going to be a police detective. Never mind my depressed economic circumstances, my limited educational opportunities, and, most significantly, here in the Deep South, the black color of my skin. I was, by God, going to be a detective. This goal was cultivated by the sheer number and variety of detective programs delivered to me by multiple radio networks. There were dozens of these programs. Among my favorites: *Dragnet, The FBI in Peace and War*, and *Yours Truly, Johnny Dollar*. These programs and so many others very much influenced me. Each of these shows embodied the essence of my idea of compassionate, fair, equitable, and just treatment when applying the law. To this day, I tune my SiriusXM satellite radio to old radio programs such as these. Becoming a detective was my dream. It was a long shot, but it was all I wanted. It would satisfy my ambition, and it would serve my community.

I wanted to be one of the good guys who came in and saved the day, making certain that the bad people were arrested and the good people were not. I was also enamored with the fact that detectives dressed sharply, a direct reaction to the traumatic experience of being called "Sloppy Bubba" and the admiration for the polished and put-together style of one of my early partners.

I also wanted to be in a position where I could give breaks to people who were in deserving situations. I learned early that law enforcement officers, particularly detectives, have discretion regarding when to arrest and when to be merciful, if the situation requires mercy. I often say to people that I hope I did not miss an opportunity to give someone a break when they deserved it. Law enforcement officers are quite often in situations where they make decisions based on their judgment and discretion in who is arrested and charged. The state attorney has discretion in who is prosecuted. And the judge has discretion in how much time a person gets if convicted—or if they are put on probation. I think the pursuit of justice allows for the fair dispensation of judgment to facilitate those processes. I wanted to be a major player in that process.

I recognized, when contemplating becoming a detective, that I very seldom, if ever, saw a Black detective. I may not have seen a Black detective, but I had a role model who helped me move from apathy to clarity in taking the next steps to my detective dreams. Lucky for me, that role model slept in my house.

⚖

Eugene Marion Glover, five years older than me, was the oldest of my siblings and a stellar athlete. He played football and basketball for the New Stanton High School Blue Devils. The best all-around athlete in the region, his peers and our neighbors thought of him as "all-world," the best high school football tight end they had ever seen.

Eugene was special. He was recruited by UCLA and by the sports programs of many other top universities. For a Black boy whose family struggled against poverty, sports were a primary ticket to a better place. Eugene bought that ticket with his skill and grit. But for him, the trip was short.

After graduating from New Stanton in 1958 and earning a full athletic scholarship, he went to Florida A&M University. Located just 165 miles west in Tallahassee, the capital of Florida, FAMU is known as one of the nation's most respected Historically Black Colleges and Universities. So off he went. And back he came.

Apparently, Eugene returned home without having attended a single class, which is a problem when you're registered in college. This was a huge surprise and disappointment for all of us. To this day, I do not entirely understand it. He once shared this story, which sheds some light on his mindset at the time.

"Me and my freshman teammates were sitting around, ragging on each other about our hometowns, with the kids from big-city Miami and Tampa asserting flippant dominance. When it came to the players from Jacksonville, one of them said, 'We all dress really sharp in Jacksonville, except Glover over there. He's from Palatka.'"

I think he just couldn't take that. Back home, he had been revered as a star athlete. They called him "Big Wop," for that was the sound he made on the field when he hit an opponent. But now he was—or thought he was—being dismissed as a rube. As I said, peer groups can be good for a maturing youth, but they often can take you down the wrong path.

So, yes, he was my role model, even considering—especially considering—this setback in his life. The reason: he did not allow it to define him. He was a good person and remained a good person, and those who knew him loved and respected him. They called him the Gentle Giant. And he was. He was a devout Christian, as am I.

No one loved and respected him more than I did. To the day he died at age sixty-eight, if Eugene told me something, I listened and responded as he desired. Among other things, his advice and contacts proved instrumental in my long-shot quest to become a police officer, and his wisdom has been the key to whatever professional success I've achieved in life.

As I look back and reflect on my life, I increasingly appreciate the importance of having a mentor, a life coach, and a willing ear. A mother, father, brother, sister, uncle, aunt, friend, minister, rabbi, or coworker. Anyone who will listen and offer counsel. It befits each of us to seek out such a person and, for the benefit of others, to become such a person.

Before my brother came home from college, I was recognized as his little brother, and I drew my neighborhood and schoolyard pride from this. He was "Big Wop," and nothing made me happier than the day the entire community started calling me "Little Wop." I vividly remember sticking out my chest and feeling a little taller. I was a proud younger brother and willingly absorbed the positive glow of my brother's accomplishments. This was both a blessing and a curse, as we soon shall see. Eugene spent forty-two years working for the city's Parks & Recreation Department at a segregated city pool for Black residents and, more so, as the manager of J. P. Small Park. Named for our beloved high school coach, this was the same complex where Eugene earned his initial fame and where I later played football.

After Eugene died from cancer in October 2006, the city honored him by naming the park's adjoining playground the Eugene M. Glover Playground. It still stands on Jacksonville's Myrtle Avenue, just a fifteen-minute walk from our childhood home.

CHAPTER 2

SCHOOL, SPORTS, JAIL

Why are you here?

Let's get this out of the way right now: I was held back during my earliest days in elementary school. It was a traumatizing event, even now, more than seventy years later. I was held back in the first grade and forced to repeat it while my classmates moved on to the second grade. Oh, they put a nicer spin on it. "Retained." That was the word they used.

To this day, I'm not certain whether being held back turned out to be beneficial or detrimental—maybe a little of both. I am certain that I was deeply embarrassed by it, even back then. I still can hear my mother's friends referring to me as "the one who was put back" right in front of me. "Put back"—an even more active, more hurtful term for what had happened. Even today, as I write this, I still remember that awful feeling of being inferior or different or less worthy than others. I don't quite know why I was held back. I just remember my teacher frequently summoning me to the front of the class and adjusting my clothes or sending me to Eugene, then in the fifth or sixth grade, so that he could straighten out his "messy brother."

I distinctly remember feeling embarrassed about my clothes being inappropriate or at least not neat. But that couldn't be all of it—you don't make a kid repeat first grade just because his clothes are a little ragged. Still, they called me "Sloppy Bubba," and I had to deal with the ridicule. The original Sloppy Bubba was a guy in our neighborhood who wore his slacks down around his butt to the derisive amusement of others. This was way before it was fashionable and was nothing more than an indication of personal sloppiness. I hated being the target of the same taunt.

Yes, being held back is still a raw spot on my soul, but as life progressed, I recognized some redeeming, shaping values of the experience. As with all lessons in leadership, we either succeed or learn. When I was challenged by forces I couldn't control, I didn't give up but instead assessed the situation and determined to do everything in my power to shift future outcomes.

Years later, when I competed for a promotion, part of my drive was a determination not to be graded as inadequate. Perseverance. Stick-to-it-ness. Get up when knocked down. Those were my North Stars as my career was unfolding and my leadership skills were developing.

Jumping back to "Sloppy Bubba" for a moment, it was a defining time in my life. I was determined never to be viewed as a sloppy or disheveled dresser.

Funny story . . . when I was a detective in the Burglary Unit, I got a spot on my shirt and decided to go home and change into a clean shirt. There was a running bet as to whether I would simply change my shirt or if I'd take a full shower and change my entire outfit. Well, the person who voted that I would shower and change my outfit won the bet. Even today, at my age, if there's a spot on my shirt and even if someone else says it looks "just fine," I will change that shirt. Every time. And if I don't, my wife will let me know about it. Many were the times when I would come to her in the morning to kiss her goodbye and she would say, "Where are you going, looking like that?" Of course, this would inspire me to change the tie or pair of socks or whatever else had attracted her, shall we say, special notice.

As I mentioned, my initial school—racially segregated, of course— was an ancient wooden structure known as Old La Villa. That building is long gone, but the name lives on. About one mile away stands La Villa School of the Arts, a revered public magnet middle school that today serves students in grades six, seven, and eight with specialized programs in arts and academics. By the time I reached the fourth grade, Old La Villa had pretty much been shuttered, and we were assigned to the more modern A. L. Lewis Elementary, which was a two-story brick building. Built in 1917, it also was segregated and smaller than you might think, but at least it looked like a conventional school. (Now somewhat worse for wear, it serves as an office complex for a group of Baptist ministers.)

I did pretty well at A. L. Lewis because I was determined never to be considered a failure again. I would go on to prove to myself and to those who had held me back that I was better than they had labeled me to be. I then moved on to James Weldon Johnson Junior High. Again a segregated school, the building was only three or so years old when I arrived there in the mid-1950s, and we benefited from its then-modern features. That place represents a special point of pride for me. Many decades later, as president of nearby Edward Waters College, I acquired my junior high alma mater and turned it into the home of the Edward Waters College Department of Teacher Education and Urban Studies. (In turn, the building's original name, which honored a respected local educator and civil rights activist, was transferred to the new James Weldon Johnson College Preparatory Middle School, which thrives to this day.)

Next up for me was New Stanton High School, where I would be following in the giant footsteps of my brother. At first, that was a bonus. Eugene was—and remains to this day—the much-heralded Stanton Blue Devil athlete, and, as I also have mentioned, that brought me plenty of attention and positive recognition. Unfortunately, that didn't last very long. By my sophomore year at New Stanton, as I resisted joining the football team or any athletic team, they started referring to me as "Sorry." A sorry kid, somehow not living up to expectations. After all, I was Eugene's little brother. Eugene, the most talented football player in the region. Eugene, who received a full scholarship to play football at Florida A&M. But I was not Eugene's talented brother; I was his lazy brother.

This was intolerable to me, but when it came to school, it was grounded in fact. The only reason I was still there was because my mother compelled me to attend, and I arrived five minutes before the opening bell and left five minutes after the closing bell. The whole notion of staying after school for football, basketball, or anything else that held absolutely no appeal was utterly foreign to me. I didn't see the need to go this far when I was already reaping the benefits of my older brother's hard work and accomplishments. Still, in my neighborhood and at my school (let's be honest, in pretty much any neighborhood and at any high school), being considered "sorry" meant that you fell short. High school is sufficiently challenging without having to deal with that reputation. So by the time I reached my junior year, I took the only path available to me and had a chat with the school's head football coach, the locally famed James P. Small, pleading with him to let me try out for the team.

Among other accomplishments, Coach Small had been instrumental in organizing the first North-South All-Star football and basketball games for Black people at a time when Jim Crow laws and lynchings still terrorized Black people in the South.

My timing was not terrific. The football team was already in spring training, preparing for the following school year, which would be my senior year. Under the best of circumstances, I would have only one season with the team. I was forced to plead my case, and finally, Coach Small relented. My just-in-time strategy worked. God's promise that He will do exceedingly and abundantly above all we can ask or think was evident in Coach Smalls's decision to allow me to participate in spring training practices. I think I made the comment, "I am Eugene Glover's brother," and I believe to this day that's what snagged his attention.

I dashed excitedly into the locker room, anticipating my cool uniform and the wonderful equipment awaiting me. Reality didn't quite match my excitement and anticipation. I almost ran into the equipment manager, who seemed annoyed and offhandedly pointed to a pile of left-over equipment. Let me rephrase that—it was more like a pile of second-hand junk piled in the middle of the floor. The equipment manager grudgingly dove into that pile and found enough equipment to create my first football uniform. It was less than ideal. My shoes were too big. I looked like a clown. My first-grade teacher would not have approved. But I had found my way. I trained exceptionally hard. Lo and behold, I made the team as a starting guard. Not only that, but I played so well that I was named the school's most outstanding offensive lineman for my exceptional ability to play every down on offense while also occasionally playing defense. I was offered a full scholarship to attend Edward Waters College. Without hesitation or reservation, I refer to this set of circumstances as divinely ordered by God. Before all this, I had not even considered going to college. I merely was fulfilling—or at least thought I was fulfilling—the mandate my mother had imposed that if I stayed in her house, I also had to stay in school. All I needed to do was graduate from high school. Turns out, I did much more.

Throughout my school years, I did not question the quality of the facilities or the actual education—mostly because I didn't have anything with which to compare it. I attended thoroughly segregated Black schools, which were funded and maintained as an afterthought. It was many years before I saw a new textbook. All the frayed books we received came from white public schools. This was something we all got used to, so it didn't seem like a big deal at the time, at least consciously. What our young minds didn't comprehend was that we deserved better. However, the implicit messaging that Black people weren't worth as much as white people became second nature to our thinking. It was yet another sign-post that we were considered second-class citizens, even second-class human beings.

As I got older and wiser, I realized that the intent was to make us feel beneath or less than who we were and who we were to become. However, the values my parents had instilled in me contributed to me using this subpar treatment as a stepping stone instead of a stumbling block.

Throughout my elementary school, junior high school, and high school years, I was a C plus or B minus student. No worse but also no better. Remember, I was not required to stay in school one minute more than necessary, and I did not. There is no question in my mind that I could have been a much better student if I had taken it more seriously and studied after I left the classroom and went home. But as long as I was making passing grades, I was not required to study at home, and I did not do so.

I do not blame my parents for this. Their formal education had been minimal. If my siblings and I managed to graduate from high school, our generation had surpassed their generation. They had done their work. I completely understand that.

Why had I resisted taking up sports until I was almost done with high school? I had a blurry, utterly wrong, and immature sense that sports and school were tickets to nowhere. In my neighborhood, the street kids—the truants—had money, girls, and respect. However, the glamorously perceived street life was always short-lived, and many who embraced that lifestyle ended up in jail or the grave many years before their time. I can recall only a few guys who took school seriously and benefited from it—one became an attorney, two became teachers, and the other was me. My mother and her insistence that we finish school saved all six of us kids from the grim fate of prison or untimely death that was often the price paid for street life.

Since my mother made it clear that truancy was not an option for me, I searched for other ways to earn some independence. I became a newsboy, and I was pretty good at it. At that time, the main newspapers in town virtually ignored the Black community. Their "colored" sections printed obituaries and little else. (In 2020, the only surviving paper— the *Times-Union*—got around to publishing an apology for essentially ignoring Ax Handle Saturday six decades earlier.) The Black newspapers were different. They were ours, and they printed all the latest stories of my community, the Black community. The weekly *Florida Star*, founded in 1951, remains in existence and still devotes itself to Jacksonville's African American population.

I sold the *Star* to local homes and hawked it on the street, keeping four cents of every fifteen-cent sale. I was able to sell as many as fifty copies in good times and make two dollars in profit. I always gave my mother fifty cents of that profit to help with household expenses. I grew up believing that when you worked, you needed to contribute to the family, and I faithfully executed my obligations. I remember the day when my mother said, "Keep the money." To her, I had realized my commitment and again, I had achieved her goal for me. I now had a deeply embedded work ethic that has endured for the rest of my life and served me well. Unlike my siblings, who never hesitated to come to me for a loan, I saved my money systematically: earn a dime and save a nickel; that was my sentiment.

After receiving my mother's blessing to keep all the money I earned, I felt motivated to expand my work efforts. I was hired to wash dishes at Morrison's Cafeteria, and because they ran a swift business, they kept me busy. I was working when I wasn't in school or at football practice. I was a pretty good kid. Yet I landed in jail during my senior year in high school, charged with the high crime of possessing two napkins while Black. Though traumatic at the time, it turned out to be one of the best things that ever happened to me.

Here's the story, all true.

I worked as a dishwasher at Morrison's Cafeteria, a popular downtown restaurant. I was seventeen and feeling pretty good about myself, with more pocket money and an enhanced work ethic.

Morrison's remained open until around nine o'clock most nights, and we'd work for another hour or so cleaning up and getting ready for the next day. One night, as I was walking home with a buddy, two police officers stopped us on the street. They were detectives—remember, all I ever wanted to be was a detective—and they apparently were checking everyone coming out of Morrison's. It seems that someone had been stealing sirloin steaks (the most expensive item on our menu). Dish room employees did not have access to steaks of any sort, much less raw steaks.

Nevertheless, the detectives stopped us, searched me, and found two napkins in my back pocket. Then they said, "Tell us who's stealing the steaks, and we'll let you go." I couldn't tell them even if I wanted to because I didn't have the faintest idea.

The result: I was charged with petty larceny for allegedly stealing two napkins. To this day, I believe that those cops probably were racist and that they would not have arrested a white kid under those same circumstances. But to be fair, I did have the napkins. I want to believe that those officers were following the letter of the law, and perhaps to some degree, they were. However, they did have access to experience and discretion in their decision-making and chose to be obtuse and rigid because they were probably racist—and there's nothing fair about that. They might have been aroused by my coworker, who also possessed a number of napkins and was giving them some lip, but still . . . two napkins in my pocket . . . and off to jail I went.

There I was, sitting in a community cell with other alleged offenders. They were bragging about their supposed accomplishments, the reasons they were in jail, and their criminal prowess. One guy was boasting—inappropriately, of course, in polite society—about how many cars he had stolen, and that won him a round of wide approval. Another guy talked about how he had robbed someone. A third guy congratulated himself on the many houses he had burglarized. All of this was met with great applause. It was as if I were at the Academy Awards for dopes. If I were to consider another way to look at it, one would not want to appear weak in a space with other criminals, so bragging about their crimes could have been a means of self-protection and self-preservation in a space where signs of weakness held horrible consequences.

I was sitting there with my head down, hoping they wouldn't ask me anything, but they finally got around to me. "Hey, buddy. What did you do?" This was what I had feared—that I wouldn't, I don't know, measure up to these guys. A piece of me, given the situation, really kind of wanted to. At that moment, I found myself wishing I had done something more criminally impressive, something that would validate my presence.

I said, "Larceny," hoping that would suffice. It didn't.

"What did you steal?" one man inquisitively asked. Uh-oh. Now I was in for it.

"Two napkins," I whispered.

That confession was repeated, loudly and forcefully, to all within earshot. The entire cell, then the adjoining cells, erupted in laughter. I was less amused, and I almost wished I had committed a more serious crime.

I was told I had one phone call I could make. This was a dilemma. You've already met my strict disciplinarian mother. She had made it clear that if any of us landed in jail, she was not coming to get us.

This was her version of a deterrent to further misdeeds. I knew I had to call home, but the probabilities were on my side. Sitting there at home were my brother, sisters, and father. I had at least a four out of five chance that someone other than my mother would answer the phone. Still, I prayed that the odds would break for me, that my mother would not answer the phone.

One ring. Another ring. Of course, it was my mother who picked up the phone. Half-crying, I told her that I was in jail. She did not say another word to me, but I heard her turn to my father and tell him to go and get me out of jail. My father, then still working as a plasterer, called his white boss, Mr. Sullivan, for help. The two of them came and bailed me out of jail.

The next morning, I had to appear at the Jacksonville Municipal Court. My father told me that someone downtown had told him I should plead guilty, and nothing further would happen to me. So there I was in Judge John E. Santora Jr.'s courtroom. Standing at my side were my father and my boss, Leon Ashby.

I ended up pleading guilty to stealing two napkins, which remains incredible to me today. While I pride myself on a reputation of trustworthiness, I humbled myself to abide by my father's advice and acquiesce to the plea, trusting that the outcome would be better for me than challenging the validity of the officers' implication of my guilt. But Mr. Ashby's explanation to the judge that we "used the napkins to wipe away our sweat" held up my value and reputation as a trusted employee, easing the burden of my imposed guilty plea. In fact, we were not allowed to go home with these napkins; I merely had forgotten they still were in my pocket.

The judge set me free and said, "I never want to see you down here again." I made good on that. I never expected this case to rear its ugly head again because for years, I thought that the judge accepted my guilty plea and vacated or suspended my sentence. However, in a tumultuous race for sheriff, my opponent released information that I had previously gone to jail. The arrest became a big headline story just before the election, and this was not considered a plus on the résumé of a potential sheriff.

While it was a temporary sting, I was vindicated when my team refuted the claim with the fact that the judge had discharged the case and negated the arrest and the charges. My opponent's attempt to slander me sparked much commentary from the voters, but not in the way he expected. The general theme was, "If this is all they can find on this guy, let's elect him." And they did. I won a three-way race with 55 percent of the vote.

It also turns out that the arrest played a major role in my becoming a police officer in the first place. And it had a lasting effect on my philosophy regarding enforcing the law: when I could give someone a break, I generally did, and I rarely regretted it. I should add that my parents never asked me how those napkins had landed in my pocket. Maybe they just were glad to get me home, but a friend once shared a more satisfying explanation: "Your mother and father knew you and knew you wouldn't steal those napkins." I have settled on that interpretation.

Life has a way of coming full circle. Some years later, Judge Santora landed himself in a major jam by making a series of racist and anti-Semitic remarks. My life has been about doing the right thing when the right thing needs to be done. I unequivocally am against any form of racism and anti-Semitism and don't make any excuses for what the judge said. Nonetheless, I felt compelled not to make any comments about what he said to avoid exacerbating the situation. This was my way of extending help, simply because he had once helped me.

Race relations can be complicated. Life can be complicated. People can be complicated; they rarely fit completely into stereotypes, especially racial stereotypes. It is my belief that every human being has a nub of goodness within—after all, we are all created in God's image.

CHAPTER 3

AX HANDLE SATURDAY

**They were everywhere. It could
have ended for me that day.**

Augusti 27, 1960. Ax Handle Saturday was one of the most frightening days of my life. I could have died that day.

Civil rights protests were reaching a high boil in many corners of the South. Jacksonville was not an exception. Still, just a high school senior who was mostly preoccupied with staying in school and keeping my job at Morrison's Cafeteria, I paid only fleeting attention to the world around me, a world on the brink of tense, major change. I was nestled in my cove, not yet mindful that change was unfolding even in my hometown, within a block or two of my workplace, and that this change was deepening while the environment was darkening.

For two weeks, young Black activists, a group of youths from the National Association for the Advancement of Colored People (NAACP), had been staging sit-in demonstrations at local lunch counters, primarily in the downtown Woolworth and W. T. Grant stores.

The choreography of racial discord went something like this: One or two members of each small group would purchase an item in the store, substantiating the obvious truth that Black dollars were welcome there, to a certain limit. Then they would occupy stools at a lunch counter— the lunch counter near the front of the store that was reserved for white customers. A separate and not equal lunch counter for Black customers was tucked into the back of each store. It wasn't about the food, of course.

"When we started the sit-in demonstrations, we wanted everyone to know eating a hot dog and drinking a Coke would not be our focus," activist Rodney Hurst later wrote in an account of his life and of that day. "Human dignity would be our fundamental focus, along with making segregation extremely expensive."

In response and in rapid succession, the store refused to serve the young African Americans. White men would line up behind them, harassing and taunting them. The store would then declare the lunch counter closed. Often the store would close entirely. Police would arrest the protestors.

Many Black demonstrators were aligned with the nonviolent NAACP. Many of the white counterprotesters were aligned with the extremely violent Ku Klux Klan.

Here is an account shared by my college roommate, Marvin Grant, who participated in many of the sit-ins:

> I was part of the NAACP Youth Council. Rodney Hurst was the president. There were about fifteen of us. We did not go into any one establishment as a group, but rather broke into small groups of four or five. We went into the lunch counters at the same busy time periods for serving lunch. The intention was for restaurants to either serve us or shut down.

We would go into the restaurant and wait for empty stools to appear and take them one after another. My group always went to Woolworth's first and then, as soon as it closed, we went to another lunch counter. We wanted to hit as many as possible at the same time to ensure maximum impact. There was no violence on our part and no police intervention; most people just stood and watched us. The strategy worked, but there were growing crowds heckling us and calling us "monkeys" and "apes," and shouting, "Send them back to Africa! Yeah, let them swim back!"

Over and over, this would occur until August 27 of that year, when the city's downtown exploded into racial violence, and Jacksonville made the national news. On that day, the focus of the protests fell upon Woolworth's, at the corner of Monroe and Hogan Streets, directly across from Hemming Park. The park was named after Charles C. Hemming, a Civil War veteran and Confederate rebel. I had walked through the park occasionally and even sat on a bench there a time or two. Due to my naivety about the symbolism of this Confederate soldier, I'd never really thought much about the enormous bronze monument that stood in the park, boasting its prowess. The feeling that stood out to me more than anything was that I knew I was sitting in a park made for white people. But the park always seemed peaceful and safe, somewhat of an oasis, so I had no inkling that it was ripe to become a haven for the violence and chaos that would ensue that day.

Morrison's, where I was working that Saturday, stood across the street from Hemming Park and kitty-corner to Woolworth's. I was one of six people on the dishwashing team. The dishes would come in from the dining rooms, one upstairs and one downstairs. Business was robust, dishes were many, and we worked steadily and hard. And so I had no idea what was happening that day outside, right in the shadow of the restaurant.

Marvin Grant shared what happened next:

Ax Handle Saturday was an exception [to the general rule]. On Saturday morning, we planned to go in early when breakfast was served and shut the lunch counters down for the whole day. I was not in attendance that day because of my part-time job. A person in my group recounted the events:

"Earlier that morning, a pickup truck pulled up to Hemming Park on the JCPenney side with barrels full of ax handles. Some people must have been waiting for the truck because they immediately went up to the truck where the ax handles were being distributed.

"Apparently, they had alerted people to come and plan on hunting and finding demonstrators, maybe have 'a little fun' with them. Frankly, they were stalking any black person in the area.

"Our group sat down in Woolworth's as usual and then the ax handlers came in, and immediately the demonstrators dispersed, fearful for their lives. With the demonstrators gone, the mob started looking for any Black person. It just did not matter. They had become an unruly crowd intent on extracting revenge. It didn't matter, at this point, who the Black person was. And the police just stood there and watched."

The violence was indiscriminate. More than two hundred white thugs, some dressed in Confederate uniforms, many also brandishing baseball bats, stalked and attacked at random—and targeted not just Black demonstrators. Old men and women accompanied by their children, shoppers, and passersby. Anyone with black skin was threatened, harassed, and beaten.

"In a surreal scene, they swung those ax handles and baseball bats at every Black person they saw," Hurst wrote.

Rodney Hurst was only sixteen years old at the time, but he had assumed the mantle of leadership as president of the local NAACP Youth Council. Many years later, Hurst described the violence this way to the *Florida Times-Union*, Jacksonville's main newspaper: "A swing, a sound, then red."

Regrets? Not really. "Even if we knew that violence was going to occur, I don't know if we would have canceled the demonstrations that day," Hurst told the *Times-Union*.

So this is what I unknowingly walked into that afternoon.

One of my responsibilities at my job was to mop the floors, so I was one of the last people—certainly, the last Black person—to leave Morrison's that day. Even so, this was earlier than it otherwise would have been. Our manager, hearing rumors and predictions of confrontation or worse, tried to protect us by sending us home relatively early, but I stayed at work until my tasks were accomplished.

I walked out of the back door, through a side alley—and into a nightmare at Hemming Park. No shoppers, no pedestrians, not even any vehicles. I looked around and saw not a single Black face. Just white police officers and white vigilantes wielding axe handles and bats. To get home, I somehow had to get past those thugs.

But...how?

There was no way to avoid them. They were everywhere.

I contemplated the best way to avoid the adrenaline-high crowd. Taking back roads, which would lead me to the outskirts of my town, giving me a much longer journey only to perhaps prolong my inevitable encounter with the indignant mob, was an option I pondered. But time was not on my side, and thinking through my escape would only give the attackers a jump start on me. In retrospect, I know I could have turned around and gone well out of my way to avoid the crowd before finding my way back home. But there was something in me that prevented me from doing this. Was it courage? Resistance? Foolhardiness?

Fifteen to twenty of the angry men quickly surrounded me, waving their axe handles and bats. They taunted me with slurs such as "boy" and "nigger."

They screamed at me. "What you doin' here?" and "Where you going?"

"Home. Where do you think I'm going?" I said in the humblest tone I could, trying to sound as nonthreatening as possible. But I could tell by the tone of their rhetorical questions that nothing I said really mattered; they were determined to execute their agenda.

Then came the blows. They started to jab at me with their bats and axe handles. Not disabling hits but menacing, prodding blows to my shoulders and legs—fortunately, nothing that would cripple or kill me. Luck? Angels? Or could it have been that they were smart enough not to send me off for good because a police officer was there? I'll never know. But I am grateful that I am here today to tell my story.

A white police officer stood just outside this circle of violence, watching indifferently and seemingly there for the entertainment value. I was dazed. The physical pain was relatively minor, largely overwhelmed by the emotional terror. It was a petrifying feeling. I remember thinking that all I'd done that day was wash dishes, mop a floor, and try to get home to my family. Why was this happening to me? I remember a fleeting opening that allowed me to run to that white police officer.

"Help! Help me, please!" I pleaded.

His unconcerned response was, "Boy, you better get out of here before they kill you."

Somehow, I did get out of there. God spared my life that day. He cleared a path for me; nothing short of divine intervention can be the reason for that. I ran the entire mile back to my house, not once looking back to see if any of the assailants were on my heels. Once I arrived home, I went straight to the room I shared with my siblings and took to my bed, weeping. I cried not because of the pain of being hit repeatedly, not even due to the fear. I cried because I was wracked with entirely inappropriate shame.

I replayed it in my mind . . . how I had run away. In my neighborhood, there was an unwritten rule: if you ran away from a fight, you were a coward. You were supposed to stand and fight. You might lose the fight, but at least you wouldn't be branded as a coward. Now, so many years later, as I think back to that experience, I realize that as a civilian, I deserved to be protected. The nonviolent protestors also deserved to be protected as they exercised their rights as citizens. I was afraid, as much as it pains me to admit that. However, the branding of cowardice and shame lay squarely on the shoulders of the spineless bullies who took to the streets to attack women and children and unarmed men and boys simply because they were Black. My survival was necessary so that my destiny could be fulfilled. What was meant to kill me only made me stronger. Even though I had no choice but to flee, I never wanted to feel that way again. I became someone who always needed to confront my fear. I never wanted someone to accuse me of not doing something because I was afraid to do it. Or doing something because I was afraid not to do it. I am convinced it was at that point in time when I became a person who runs to the fire, not a person who runs from it. I wanted to spend the rest of my life striving for justice.

I have lived my life confronting fear—fear of failing, fear of not measuring up, fear of unfamiliar challenges, fear of losing my life—and overcoming those fears. And I never did forget—or even can forget—that it could have ended for me that day. Another instance of my life being spared, as I came very close to being murdered by a mob while a police officer stood by and watched, like a fan at a ball game. That should have been enough to deter me from becoming a police officer, but it did the opposite.

I would become a police officer by God's grace, and I would work for the balance of my life to rid the force of racist cowards. But first, an opportunity to attend college beckoned . . . twice . . . though I only took the opportunity seriously once. . .for real.

I learned later that the mob assault was covered prominently by the *New York Times*, the *Los Angeles Times*, the national television networks, and many other media outlets. The front page of the *New York Times* read: "Angry bands of club-swinging whites clashed with Negroes in the streets of downtown Jacksonville today." But the *Florida Times-Union*, then and now Jacksonville's primary source of news, saw no reason to dwell on or significantly report the events of that day. Outrageously, the *Times-Union's* brief story, buried inside the newspaper, focused solely on a few injuries reported by white participants. Only the *Florida Star*, the Black community's paper that I once hawked as a kid, reported fully on the events of that day.

It wasn't until sixty years later that the *Times-Union* apologized for its passive treatment of the significant events that took place on that horrific Saturday. It wasn't just that they didn't bother to give credence to the story at the time—they didn't bother to address it for many years to follow. I feel it was a disservice to the people of Jacksonville, white and Black, because they depended on the newspaper to keep them informed of current events—ideally, without bias. However, it was obvious there was bias, and I'd even go as far as saying they were complicit, which was why they refused to give light to the event or condemn it then and during subsequent years.

On August 21, 2020, the newspaper finally offered an apology: "The *Florida Times-Union* committed an act of journalistic malpractice so egregious that it deserves a formal apology." I believe the newspaper showed courage in admitting their wrongdoing, although I still wonder: Would they have reported it had I been killed that day? I'll never know.

On June 9, 2020, in the wake of local and nationwide protests of the slaying of George Floyd by police officers in Minneapolis, the Confederate monument in Hemming Park was removed after having stood there for 122 years. Two months later, the park's name was changed. No longer does it honor a traitorous Confederate. Now it is called James Weldon Johnson Park in honor of the famed Black writer, diplomat, and civil rights activist born in Jacksonville. (One of my highest honors came upon my retirement as sheriff in 2003, when Pastor Gary L. Williams of First Baptist Church of Mandarin said, "Nat Glover's name will one day be written next to James Weldon Johnson and [civil rights leader] A. Phillip Randolph in Jacksonville history books." It was a prophecy that proved true. The names *Nathaniel Glover* and *James Weldon Johnson* are both recorded in Jacksonville history as "Great Floridians," a designation made by the governor to recognize notable contributions made to the state of Florida.) A historical marker stands in the park now, reminding all who pass by of Ax Handle Saturday. It says, in part:

> *Many of the youth were injured, while others sought safety at the adjacent Snyder Memorial Methodist Church. Although not the beginning of the Jacksonville Civil Rights movement, this conflict was a turning point. It awakened many to the seriousness of the African American community's demand for equal rights, equal opportunity, human dignity, and respect. It inspired further resolve in supporters to accomplish these goals.*
>
> *Within the decade, lunch counters were integrated, Duval County public schools began desegregating, four African Americans were elected to City Council, and segregation of public accommodations, including parks, restrooms, and water fountains, ended.*

Often, adversity and events that seem damaging and troubling turn out to be so instructive and influential that they truly shape you into a better person. Each of these lessons learned informs and quite often shapes the person you are to become. The damaging nature of trauma is not the thing I value, but the opportunity to respond to adversity with directness, bravery, and integrity resonates with my moral compass. My only goal on Ax Handle Saturday was to stay alive; however, the result was that I would lead a life to effect meaningful change so that no other Black boy would experience the terror I did on that day.

CHAPTER 4

HIGHER EDUCATION

If at first you don't succeed ...

If my parents ever dreamed of sending me to college, they certainly kept that to themselves. It is difficult to speak or write about the value of education without indulging in hackneyed banalities or bromides. Right about now, you're probably expecting a "but." Well, here it is. But ... I have seen the difference education can make. I have experienced it. I have lived it. And I believe I can say that others have benefited from my experience, from the difference education has made in my life, and, partially as an affirmative consequence, in their lives.

As I've mentioned, moving on to college—heck, even just graduating from high school—was not a top-tier ambition among my neighborhood contemporaries. Again, I can think of only a few of us who attained a college education—two guys who became teachers, another who became an attorney, and me. Remember, becoming a police detective was my only goal. College simply was not on my radar screen, and, unfortunately, I didn't comprehend the value of a college education. College was an expense for families that had the means, and my family certainly did not. To be honest, if we'd had to pay to attend high school, I'm not sure that any of us would have gone.

Blessed with only partial elementary school education, my parents focused primarily on just keeping me and my brother and sisters in school and generally off the streets until we graduated from high school. My parents' focus paid off, and every one of us graduated from high school. My younger sister, Shirley, and I went on to graduate from college. As fate would have it, I presented and signed her degree as president of the college. They succeeded in granting their children better educations than they had been given. I ought to have looked around proudly at what our family had accomplished in a single generation, but I was too busy comparing my empty pockets to all the stuff my friends in the streets had.

As I said, growing up in the ghetto, I was iron to the magnets that were on the streets. Some of those guys had money in their pockets, cars at the ready, and girls in the front (and sometimes the back) seats. To my pubescent eyes, it looked like they were experiencing a pretty good life— and they weren't going to school. Given my mother's insistence—"You're going to school as long as you're living in this house"—my objective was to do the minimum necessary to avoid getting kicked out of high school. To me, that seemed quite enough. Back then, a high school diploma was the only educational requirement for becoming a police officer. So my grades were mediocre, just enough to keep me in school until I could collect that piece of paper required by police recruiters. I didn't have anyone at home—or even in school—who was encouraging me to think educationally beyond high school.

But my post–high school aspirations changed rather dramatically after I joined the football team. As is still the case today for African

Americans and other minorities, athletics was the key to unlocking utterly unanticipated opportunities, and that's what happened for me. After excelling as a high school football offensive lineman, I was offered a full scholarship to attend Edward Waters College, just one mile from my home on Minnie Street. Honestly, I only understood that I was good enough to play college football when offered that scholarship.

One day after practice, I was walking out of the locker room when I was approached by my coach, who introduced me to a smiling man who shook my hand robustly and asked if I had a moment to talk. This man shocked me when he announced that I was being considered for outstanding offensive lineman of the year. I wondered, *How could this be?* After all, I only started playing football so that others would stop calling me "Sorry."

He then asked, "Nat, have you ever considered going to college?"

Caught off guard by the question, I stood there in silence, quickly trying to decide if it was something I'd considered. Unlike my team-mates, college was not on my radar.

He didn't wait for me to respond before continuing, "Because Edward Waters College would love to offer you a full scholarship."

Still stunned, I began to let the flood of new possibilities wash over me. And just like that, I decided. "I'd like that very much!" I replied.

Eager about the opportunity I'd never considered but was now my reality, I couldn't wait to tell my mother and Eugene. My parents and siblings were equally surprised and supportive, recognizing that this was potentially a ticket to a better place. My mother's reaction to the news was direct yet warm: "You've got to do this!" I remember my siblings' excitement—behaving as if they were the ones headed off to college. The air of our house was filled with joy. Our hearts sang quietly. Our bodies hummed in tune. Smiles adorned our faces, and dreams of a brighter future glistened in our eyes.

A little later, we will discuss at great length and depth Edward Waters College—now, to my everlasting pride, officially elevated to and known as Edward Waters University—and my later roles there, but for now, please know that it was and remains a small but crucial centerpiece of higher learning for minorities in the Jacksonville area.

Founded in 1866 as Florida's first HBCU (Historically Black Colleges and Universities), Edward Waters still serves about one thousand full-time students attending five bachelor's degree programs. The college is a member of the United Negro College Fund, and it remains associated with the African Methodist Episcopal (AME) Church.

The importance of Edward Waters and the nation's other HBCUs to minority communities cannot be overstated. Here is how Don Calloway, vice president of equity, inclusion, and impact at a renewable energy company and a former state representative in Missouri, put it in a piece he wrote in 2021 for the *Washington Post* advocating greater public and private support for HBCUs:

> *There is no further debate over the relative value or enduring necessity of Historically Black Colleges and Universities. HBCUs produce global leaders who just happen to be Black. Attending an HBCU was the one time in my life that my success or my failure was based on my personal merit and completely detached from notions of race. The freedom to think, learn, grow, and lead without the reductive lens of race and racism during one's formative years has the power to springboard young Black Americans to unprecedented heights of achievement.*

So Edward Waters College, named for the third bishop of the African Methodist Episcopal Church, appeared to be my immediate destination.

I graduated from high school in 1961, and still a little startled, I started to make plans to attend college. My stated goal was to become a teacher, but in my heart, I knew that I still yearned to become a police detective and would find some way to achieve that.

Why a teacher, even as an interim objective? For African Americans then, and even in some quarters today, becoming a teacher was one of the few ways to step into a genuine profession. Teacher, lawyer, nurse, maybe even a physician. Securing a place within these professions meant you could become a professional and transition from living in a shotgun house to a much nicer house with a car or two in the garage. Other than that, you would be confined to the life of a laborer—or something much worse.

Most of my teammates had elected to major in education and aimed to become teachers. My goal wasn't particularly along those lines; I knew in my heart of hearts that I wanted to become a police officer. However, the college didn't have a criminal justice program, and I knew I needed to elect a field of study. So for the purpose of choosing my major and course schedule, I elected education as my core.

Preseason football practices started about two weeks before college classes began, and I dove into them with excitement and genuine expectations of good things to come. The Edward Waters Tigers were a class act, with a reputation of excellence, almost always in contention for the small-school Southeastern Athletic Conference championship. But, alas, it was not to be. Not for me. Not quite yet. Being on my own at college was not for me. I just didn't want to do this. I didn't have the motivation to be a part of any college community. Being on campus felt cold and lonely. I wanted to be home with my family and friends. Playing football no longer interested me; it had served its purpose. I now yearned for the nostalgic warmth and comfort of my former life.

Leaving college was not the best decision I ever made. Subconsciously, perhaps I was following in Eugene's steps when he had left FAMU a few years earlier. However, I can't say this occurred to me at the time of my decision, and honestly, I don't believe it was a driving factor. I may have even used the excuse that my sister Bessie was enduring serious health issues that were straining my family's financial and emotional resources.

The plain truth, and I can admit it today, was that I just wasn't ready or committed enough for college.

Given that the football scholarship was the sole factor motivating me to attend college, I probably was not as committed to higher education as I should have been. So instead of blocking and tackling and studying, I ended up at age nineteen lifting, dragging, and pushing heavy furniture as a laborer for Suddath Moving and Storage. After a while of performing the strenuous labor of furniture moving, I decided to ask my boss for a promotion to truck driver. Surprisingly, he said no. Struck by his candor, I couldn't understand why someone who had previously praised my hard work would suddenly shun my ambition to do more work for him. But his no wasn't a simple no. He also said, "You need to go back to college." This statement rocked me and became the catalyst I needed to get myself back in school. Now I understand what he was saying was, "Get yourself an education, or else you'll be destined for a life of backbreaking, low-paying work, and you are destined to do more than that."

My philosophy is that you can always find an excuse not to do something you're not committed to. But if you're really committed, you'll find good reasons to pursue the objective. One opportunity my moving job did afford me was that I got to see how other people lived, including officers assigned to Jacksonville's numerous military bases. They had really nice homes on the beachfront, which warmed me up to the notion that this could be me if I got my butt back in school. Maybe one day, I could have a house or a condo on the beach. This, like travel, was an opportunity to expand my knowledge of what was possible and then imagine it for myself. Exposure to different people, ideas, and ways of life is transformational. That's why it's really important that people not stay in their isolated bubbles.

Meanwhile, something else was nagging at me, something based on my traumatic experience on Ax Handle Saturday. As you recall, I ran home that day. While most people applaud and support my decision to flee the violent mob, they don't sympathize with the fact that running made me feel like a failure or a coward. I know deep down that I'm neither of those things, but the simple truth is that running that day catapulted me into vowing never to run away from anything ever again. I would do whatever I had to—even if I had to do it afraid. So my plan was to go back to college, afraid and barely committed. Completing school and not running away was my objective. Well, that's how I was beginning to feel about my premature departure from college. I didn't want to say or even think for the rest of my life that I was afraid to have given that a decent try. As a result, a little less than a year after dropping out, I swallowed some pride, returned to the Edward Waters campus, introduced myself to Clifford "Jack" Paul, the then new football coach, and basically begged for another chance.

Coach Paul didn't know me. He didn't even have to hear me out. But I believe he was divinely placed at our school because his ambition was primed to give second chances. His strategy for securing talent that most other coaches would overlook gave him the edge at building a winning team. To give you a bit of insight into Coach Paul's extended grace, which I believe is worth sharing here, there were two young men previously accused, indicted, and sentenced to death on rape charges. Both young men survived their fate and, due to a set of circumstances, were released from prison. They were both subsequently chosen by Coach Paul to play football at Edward Waters College, to be a part of a winning team, and to be given a chance at redemption. He gave me that same chance. It was all I needed, at least at that time. Just one more chance, and it was granted to me.

I was back on the team in time for the fall 1962 season and the beginning of a remarkable three-year run by Coach Paul and the Edward Waters Tigers in which we won twenty-three games and lost only three. I ended up playing four years of football there, and in my fourth year, the team won seven games and lost three. But the most important thing was that I was back in college.

During my sophomore year at Edward Waters, on September 14, 1963, I married my neighborhood sweetheart, Doris Janelle Bailey. At that point, we were already parents of my eldest daughter, Clementine, and Doris was pregnant with our son, Michael.

Doris and her father lived on the 800 block of Minnie Street, just across Logan Street and not far from my house at 734 Minnie Street. Her dad was rather protective of her and didn't allow her to come out and play with us very often, but we were in some of the same classes in school. One thing led to another, and we fell in love.

When Doris became pregnant and had Clementine, it just wasn't viewed in our circles as scandalous or even unusual. It just was the way things sometimes happened. We moved into my parents' home, and that was that. It never entered my mind that we might not get married eventually, and when we learned that we were expecting Michael, that seemed like the right time. So a couple of months before he was born, we drove up to Folkston, Georgia, about forty miles east of Jacksonville, went before a justice of the peace, and got married. I was twenty years old. Doris also was twenty. We were parents of a daughter with a son on the way. We continued to live with my parents until I finished college. They were extremely under-standing and caring. We were family.

A year after becoming a married man, during my junior year in school in 1963, I was appointed co-captain of the football team. When the coach called me in to tell me I was being tapped as co-captain, I thought he was talking to someone behind me, so I turned to congrat-ulate whoever that was—that's how surprised I was. Looking back, I realize that this is when I truly started to refine my leadership skills.

Running conditioning drills and pregame warm-up routines. Encouraging teammates during games. Promoting good sportsmanship.

All of these, and more, are part of a team captain's portfolio. I hadn't thought about serving in that position, but the coach appointed me, and my teammates were supportive. And we had a heck of a run. We went 7–2 in 1962, 7–1 again in 1963, and 9–0 in 1964 (as we piled up 498 points to our opponents' 20 points). So during three of my four years on the team, we compiled a record of twenty-three wins and only three losses. We won the Southeastern Athletic Conference title in each of those three years, and Coach Paul parlayed those accomplishments into a new job as head coach at the larger Texas Southern University.

In addition, back in the classroom, I got somewhat serious—though not serious enough—about my schoolwork and was elected vice president of the Social Sciences Club. The pattern continued. People saw leadership qualities in me that I did not see in myself. This would be a frequently repeated phenomenon as adult life rushed toward and enveloped me. My full scholarship included a work-study requirement. Unfortunately, my luck ran out when it came to the "work" part, and I wish I had given more attention to the "study" part. Regarding work, I was responsible for cleaning the men's restrooms. Believe me; you have not fully comprehended the term "work" unless you have cleaned a nasty, unsanitary, hot, dirty men's restroom.

Regarding study, my social sciences program included history, and I really enjoyed that subject—and still do. Studying history and the people who took risks and made history, such as Abraham Lincoln and the Wright brothers, serve as motivation for me. I'm embarrassed to report that I studied very little in college. I had natural ability, but to this day, I am saddened when I realize that if I had invested more effort, I could have learned even more and emerged as a straight-A student. Still, college taught me that once you obtain a body of knowledge, you almost have a duty to shoulder opportunities that will advance society.

Two of my teachers in particular greatly influenced me at Edward Waters College. One was Dorothy Gaither, who encouraged me to run for vice president of the Social Sciences Club. She was among the very first people who encouraged me to remain confident in my unique abilities and thoughts, even if those thoughts were different from those held by others. Everyone needs someone—a champion—who believes in their abilities, a crucial engine as we ride the wave of life. Ms. Gaither was mine.

Coach Paul was my second great champion at Edward Waters. He inspired me to grow into my leadership capability when he appointed me co-captain of the football team during my junior year.

On the social front, I pledged to the Omega Psi Phi fraternity, mostly because I was told that it was the most difficult to get into and because of the impressive qualities of its members already in the fraternity. Founded in 1911 at Howard University in Washington, DC, Omega Psi Phi was the first international fraternity ever created at an HBCU. Its initials represent the Greek phrase, "Friendship is essential to the soul."

Among its notable members are civil rights leaders Roy Wilkins, Jesse Jackson, Vernon Jordan, and Benjamin Hooks; writer Langston Hughes; musician and band leader Count Basie; comedian Steve Harvey; basketball stars Michael Jordan and Shaquille O'Neal; publisher Earl Graves; and many others.

At my frat, I was made sergeant at arms, an apparent recognition of the abilities that would carry me to my professional law enforcement career. I shared a dorm room with Marvin Grant, a childhood friend with a photographic memory, and the fellow you already met through his description of Ax Handle Saturday. Guys used to come to our dorm room to study for tests—and not just because we had the dorm's only television and record player. Marvin says they just liked hanging out with us, and to be honest, I found myself able to help them prepare for their tests. They called our room the command post because Marvin was the basileus of Omega Psi Phi and president of the Student Government Association, and I was his lieutenant and co-captain of the football team.

Many of my friends and colleagues at EWC also went on to have exceptional careers. That's a story in itself, a group of poor Black boys in the 1950s, all destined for college and greatness. Marvin earned advanced degrees from EWC, Florida A&M, and the University of Florida, where he earned a doctoral degree. He taught in the Duval County school system for ten years before moving on to a multifaceted and distinguished career in higher education, including teaching and prestigious administrative positions at several universities. He has served on many boards throughout the country, twice was named Outstanding Black Educator in Florida Higher Education, and was appointed by then governor Bob Graham to the Florida Board of Architecture and the Florida Board of Vocational and Technical Education.

In due course, I graduated from Edward Waters with a bachelor's degree in social science, as close as I could come to a teaching degree. Later, I earned a master's degree in education from the University of North Florida, a certificate from the Federal Bureau of Investigation National Academy, and two honorary degrees.

But I still yearned to become a police officer, something my peers could not understand. A police detective rather than a teacher? They couldn't see it. But becoming a police officer was embedded in my soul. I could live with failing to become a police officer. I could not live without at least *trying* to become a police officer. I knew I had to become a police officer before becoming a detective, which was undoubtedly my ultimate goal. And I just wanted to do good for society. I also could not forget the image of my neighborhood and the multiple houses at which illegal moonshine was being sold. I, along with others in the neighborhood, often saw police officers going in and coming out of those houses without taking any enforcement actions. It was clear to me that this was unacceptable. I wanted to be one of the good police officers who changed that image. But I knew the challenge of becoming a police officer as an African American would be difficult. It was generally known in the Black community that the city only wanted a certain number of Black police officers. There were many stories about African Americans who took the police examination and later were told they had not met the requirements. The perception was clear that this was a pervasive control strategy.

As a result, I was always a proponent of what I call my four Ps: *plan, prepare, persevere,* and *pray,* which allowed me to reflect on difficult challenges and try to overcome them. And clearly, being an African American with a record of having been arrested as a young man made the goal of becoming a police officer all the more difficult. But that was not a deterrent; it was more of a challenge that I was prepared to take on. So becoming a police officer, always my goal and my ambition, met the requirement of the first P—to *plan.* Then, the achievement of having earned a college degree became the fulfillment of the second P—to *prepare.* When I had to overcome obstacles in the police department, I had to rely on that third P—to *persevere.* And, finally, when all else failed, I turned to my fourth P and learned to *pray.* We will see how that worked out later.

CHAPTER 5

ROOKIE POLICE OFFICER

Your racism makes me ashamed
to be a police officer.

The main reason I wanted to become a police officer, and specifically, a detective, was that I'd be positioned to assess and make the discretionary decision to arrest or not to arrest someone when appropriate. When I think back to my unduly harsh arrest for having the two napkins in my pocket, while the officers were acting well within their systemic right to arrest me, I wholeheartedly believe that they could have chosen the option of not arresting me for doing something far from sinister or even what could be considered noncriminal. This stretch of their duty became poignant in my gut, and from that moment, I wanted to become the kind of officer who would see things with my eyes wide open. If I had been the arresting officer that day, I would have let the young man go.

To quote English jurist Sir William Blackstone, "Better that ten guilty persons escape than that one innocent suffer." These words capture the essence of my approach to law enforcement, defining the type of officer and detective I have always wanted to become.

So where was I? Ah yes, my unrelenting drive to become a police officer. Unyielding or not, this drive immediately bumped into two road-blocks: the color of my skin and that frustratingly ridiculous arrest over the napkins. Put another way, I am Black and had a jail record. It was widely known that an arrest record disqualified pretty much anyone—particularly a Black man—from becoming a police officer.

In life, the people who love and care for you have the greatest intentions when giving you advice, especially when they believe they are protecting you from hurt, harm, danger, or disappointment. My goals were what some may have called lofty. I not only wanted to join the police force, but I also wanted to be a detective. This was always my dream, and I was ready to press forward. The general theme and consensus from some people close to me was that I was wasting my time. Some said, "Don't even go there!" The concern was twofold. First, the common belief in the Black community was that when Black men took the police officer exam and passed, they were often told they failed. Second, they were concerned about my arrest record.

Nevertheless, I submitted my application. It soon became evident that the naysayers were right. Nothing happened, which frankly was not much of a surprise.

The history of Black participation in Jacksonville law enforcement was problematic. The first Black officers in Jacksonville's modern history weren't hired until 1950, when six local candidates were sent to a separate (but not equal) training academy within the Wilder Park playground complex in the Black part of town. And, coincidentally or not, it was in 1966 that I joined the force against all odds. Sure, I had a college degree, unlike many whites who had successfully applied, but I also had that arrest on my record—and that, along with my skin color, trumped anything and everything else. But once again, the Lord stepped in.

After my brother, Eugene, dropped out of college, he worked at that segregated city pool, which I mentioned earlier, and he had befriended one of the city's few Black officers, a fellow named Marvin Young. As I pondered my next move, there I was, a married man with two children, possessing a college degree, yet with no apparent way to achieve my lifelong dream. Eugene summoned me to the pool, saying he had spoken with Marvin about my situation and wanted the two of us to meet. Now, remember, my older brother and I had the type of relationship where if he told me something, I listened and responded as expected. So I went to the pool and told Marvin the story of my ambition and that unfortunate arrest in my past. Marvin was shocked and more than a little suspicious. He thought there must have been more to my story than I related, but he swiftly came to believe me. He said, "I know the mayor. Let's go see him."

"Now?" I replied.

He said, "Yes, now."

Sure, I thought, *you know Mayor Lou Ritter, and you and I are just going to go down there right now and walk right in, and everything will be just fine. Yeah, right.* As a Black man, you are not used to having people with such connections and relationships. It also was common in my community for someone to exaggerate those capabilities. I was understandably cynical. But I was wrong. We headed directly to city hall. I wasn't even dressed properly, but there we were, emerging from the elevator in city hall and striding into Mayor Ritter's office. Even now, looking back at it, it has something of a dreamlike quality. Or maybe a nightmare because I still suspected that we were going to get tossed right back out again. But the mayor's secretary smiled at Marvin, jumped up to greet him, and said, "How is your family?" *Good Lord*, I thought. *Marvin really does know the mayor. This really is happening.*

"This young man is a college graduate and wants to join the police force," Marvin told Mayor Ritter. "But there's a situation you should know about," Marvin said, asking me to tell the mayor the story. The mayor listened intently, then shook his head.

I wasn't able to decode the mayor's body language. Marvin went on to have a more intimate discussion with the mayor, and I wondered whether the mayor understood my compelling story.

And then the conversation ended, and Marvin and I left Mayor Ritter's office. Marvin seemed pleased, but nothing really happened for a couple of weeks. And then, bingo! Police Captain William "Bing" Crosby came to my house and said he was investigating my suitability as a potential police officer. Once again, I told him the story of my arrest.

He said, "I will help you." And he did.

Soon I was summoned to take a series of tests: psychological, physical agility, and IQ. I passed them all and was offered a slot in the police academy. I was on my way.

Somehow, I think my arrest served as the catalyst for my eventual acceptance by the police department. I believe that neither Marvin nor Mayor Ritter would have batted an eye at my situation if it had not been for my arrest. Their advocacy on my behalf was predicated on undoing a wrong that had been done to me, and the divine intervention of the Lord ensured that I ended up traveling the path He had laid. To this day, I have photos of Marvin Young and Mayor Lou Ritter as part of the home screen on my cell phone, so I can remind myself of how they determined what was right and how their selfless acts helped me reach my first goal.

But something still nagged at me, and it persisted for decades. How, exactly, had this happened? How was the way cleared for a young Black man, even with a college degree but also with an arrest on his record, to enter the police academy? Was there something more? I think it was the college degree that provided the edge. As I thought about their conversation, Officer Marvin Young kept referring to me as a college graduate when he talked to the mayor. I think that made a difference.

Soon after I was allowed to take the police academy entrance exams, the Ku Klux Klan apparently burned a cross on Mayor Ritter's front lawn. This may not have had anything to do specifically with me—it likely was related to the overall perception that the mayor was "too liberal." The Deep South does not easily surrender its racism, a lesson I was to absorb repeatedly from the moment I entered the police academy to even now.

By 1955, twenty-seven Black officers were on the force, all of them reporting to white officers and prohibited from arresting white suspects. They all were confined to foot duty—no patrol cars for Black officers. Finally, about 1967 or 1968, the force was integrated. Black and white officers could now ride along as partners; this represented significant progress to me. Having only been on the force for a little over a year, I was honored to be selected as one of the first Black officers to have a white partner.

⚖

Rookie training included a demanding fifteen-week training course at the police academy and one year of probationary service on the street, monitored by a number of senior partners. It was a learning environment in which a probationary officer became familiar with the department's policies and procedures. The general and widely understood policy was that if you did anything questionable and couldn't make it through your first year without problems, you were gone. The department didn't want to invest in you any further. So as an incoming rookie, I initially had to surmount that year of probation, during which I could be fired for virtually anything. I almost didn't make the cut, even before I sat down for my first class at the academy.

As the agency was assembling enough entrants to justify a new class, it was my understanding that the department was having problems finding applicants who could pass the IQ test they were giving. The test required a minimum score of 110. In the room when I took the test, there were 121 applicants, and only 7 made the required score. I think my police academy class was the last class that was required to take the IQ test. But I passed the test, and my first assignment was to serve as a police emergency communications officer. Basically, these are the people who take calls from the public or dispatch officers when required. It is an important, if often overlooked, job, given that it often serves as the initial point of contact between the public and law enforcement officers.

During this brief period, though by now a married man with two children, I still felt no need to shave. At most, I had a little fuzz under my chin. That was it. That was enough, however, to offend my white supervisor. He reported me as violating the official dress code. His boss called me in and ordered me to shave. I said I would, and that was that, though he also counseled me to be patient about these humiliating episodes. Those, too, would end. Just be patient, he said generously, and you will be in the police academy. He also said (and I will never forget his words): "I know you didn't come here to become a glorified telephone operator."

It is important to note that this supervisor also was white. Even though there was pervasive racism in the department at that time, not everyone exhibited blatant racism. I came to believe that people are individuals and should be judged as such.

In retrospect, my experience at the police academy was quite positive. My class produced two eventual leaders of the entire department—Sheriff Jim McMillan and his successor, me. I was the only African American in the class, which did not seem to be an issue, with one notable exception.

My class included two female cadets, one of them from California. Our white commanding officer, a police lieutenant, thought she and I had become too friendly, and this had devastating consequences for her. He never said anything directly to me about this, but she eventually told me what had happened, and then everything made sense. Back then, we had to demonstrate competency in water safety by learning how to rescue someone in distress. The police academy was located on McDuff Avenue, and the practice pool was on Hendrix Avenue, about six miles away.

One of my female classmates and I generally rode to that pool in my car. I imagine that you're starting to see where this is going. One day, the lieutenant called me into his office. He asked me, in general, how I was doing. Then he wondered aloud how my family was adjusting to the thought of me becoming a police officer. I thought this was a peculiar question, but I didn't think much more about it. I just thought they were just conducting one-on-one interviews. This technically was true, though it turned out that the only interviewees were me and the female classmate from California. Before long, she asked me if the lieutenant also had spoken to me. I shared with her the content of that brief discussion.

She said "they"—including the lieutenant—also had called her in. They did not say much other than to tell her, "Keep your a-- out of his car and find another way to get to the pool." She was clearly upset. That ended our mutual, perfectly innocent rides.

I was surprised that riding with a female colleague was unacceptable. Our carpooling was known for quite some time, so when it was questioned, I was caught off guard. I won't say it was a big deal to me. I easily separated myself, and we both remained focused and graduated from the academy. I became a uniformed officer. She was assigned to the detective division. We moved through our probationary year. I made it. She did not. She was fired before she completed her probationary period.

I believe the timing was intentional because after making it through the probationary period, she would have had civil servant protection, which would have required them to show probable cause for terminating her. I heard that they fired her because she lied on her application about having occasional fainting spells, which she apparently did. It's striking that she was allowed to go through the academy and be assigned to the detective unit before they made this determination. I believed then— and I believe now—that she was fired as retribution for riding in my car (to that damn pool). As I said, the Deep South does not surrender itself easily.

In my early years as a police officer, Jacksonville, like many American cities, was shaken and ravaged by what were called "race riots." In 1969, a particularly savage riot erupted in the predominantly Black neighborhood that ran along Florida Avenue. Known as the Eastside Riot, it was triggered by the shooting of a Black resident by a white cigarette salesman who thought, probably erroneously, that his car was being burglarized. In the end, two people were wounded by gunfire, eleven were arrested, and the once-busy commercial center was burned and looted. It never fully recovered.

At the time, some in the police department believed the strategy should be to contain the rioters in their own neighborhood. Even as looting and arson flared, the area was cordoned off and we just watched as the riot ran its course. When everything calmed down, we entered the area.

In the following weeks, as was the standard operating procedure, a training officer debriefed a group of us about what we had seen and how we had responded. Here are some of the comments those officers expressed during that briefing:

> "The rioters were back-to-back. We were right to let them tear down their own neighborhood."

"Let them tear down their own communities unencumbered, so no officers are hurt."

"Officers don't want to intervene in these situations."

"No officer wants to get hurt in these particular situations."

"We should have gone in and arrested all the looters. They were committing a felony offense and should have been taken to jail."

"If I had a machine gun, I would have just mowed them down."

Our training officer allowed each officer to express themself. In hindsight, that was a smart move on his part because it exposed this kind of poison to sunlight. But some of the comments were so vicious that I was shaken to the core. I was shocked and nearly speechless. I took it as long as I could, and then I raised my hand and said, "You mean to say we are supposed to be police officers, and we are willing to mow them down and take their lives over something they are stealing?"

The overwhelming answer was affirmative. As police officers, they said, we had the right to use deadly force even for a felony.

By now, I was outraged. I almost was at the point of tears. I could not hold back. "Your racism makes me ashamed to be an officer. I am mortified by your comments."

I was so angry that the training officer halted the increasingly heated discussions and imposed a cooling-off period. We all went outside. The officers gathered into their usual cliques. I stood alone, trying to calm down.

Finally, a seasoned veteran officer approached me and said, "You know, Glover, most of the people in the room agreed with you. But what you said and how you said it prevented some people who agreed with you from saying anything." It's a pity that the officer didn't critique the murderous tones of my colleagues. Nobody who theoretically agreed with me spoke up—because it was too perilous to go against the flow of racist anger.

At the time, the officer's comments didn't make me feel better, but upon reflection, it made so much sense. To this day, I try to practice being calm in situations that may be chaotic. And overall, this strategy has served me well. When you speak loudly and emotionally, people tend to sit back and allow you to say what you have to say and then move on too often without even considering your comments. To be heard, having a sense of composure is far more effective than expressing righteous anger. More people will be willing to listen, process the information, and perhaps even agree with you and support your position. This is a life-altering lesson that I tried to consciously practice throughout my career.

⚖

My time as a probationary rookie had both highs and lows. A moment of levity came when I handled a report of a prowler outside a home at 3:00 a.m. The female resident who had reported the incident answered my knock on the door. Despite the hour, she was not dressed in a nightgown. Instead, she was wearing her Sunday best—dress, hair, and makeup all impeccable—at 3:00 a.m. This should have been my first clue that something was wrong with this picture. She invited me in and began telling me about the prowler. I was very concerned for her safety and wanted to catch this guy immediately. She said she saw him peeking through her window. I listened intently and took careful, detailed notes. She was precise and articulate. She said he was five feet ten and a half inches tall and weighed 170 pounds and that when she spotted him, he took off and ran down the street, taking the first left and the second right.

Huh? How could she know all these details? I asked her, "How could you, from inside your house, see him make these turns?" She said, "I didn't see him. I got the signals from outer space. They come in through my hair."

I didn't want to insult or challenge her. Instead, I told her in jest, "I see. You got the message from outer space and above the clouds. Oh my goodness. I'm afraid we don't have jurisdiction above the clouds. That's the FBI."

About two days later, I was standing in the police building talking to two officers when two plainclothes officers walked over and asked if I was Glover. I said that I was. "Well, I'm Williams from the FBI," one of the men said, "and we owe you one." In other words, the lady had evidently gone to the local office of the FBI and reported the signals that she was receiving. It became clear that the FBI agents were there on other business, but they took the opportunity to make certain I got that message. I also knew they were just kidding as well. Message received. You do have to be careful about what you say to people who have mental challenges. I certainly didn't want it to come across like I was making fun of her. I was merely trying to tactfully disengage from the call.

Along a similar vein, one day, Jerome (Jerry) Spates, one of my best friends who was also a former high school classmate of mine and one of the few other Black officers on the force, and I encountered a fellow who began saying strange things. I said aloud, "Twenty-seven," which is the police signal for an emotionally disturbed person. Spates said, "10–4," the police signal for acknowledgment. The man immediately responded, with complete misunderstanding and some indignation, "I'm not twenty-seven! I'm thirty-two years old!"

These incidents, and many others, illustrate a perennial problem for law enforcement officers: for at least a decade before these encounters occurred and years after, many states emptied their treatment institutions of mentally ill patients. This is a challenge to tackle because the problem isn't simple. In 1967, just as I was learning the ropes, California—led by then governor Ronald Reagan—was releasing mentally ill patients and abolishing their involuntary institutionalization. The assertion was that such institutions too often were inhumane, though many believed the real motivation was to save money. It's a civil rights challenge, a humane treatment challenge, and—in the interests of law enforcement—an equipping issue. Penalization and incarceration are not solutions to mental illness, just as a lack of treatment is insufficient.

Florida's policies were not much better until 1972 when the Baker Act was passed. It permitted the involuntary commitment and examination of emotionally disturbed people, but only for seventy-two hours. After that, even today, depending on the findings, many such people are released back to the streets.

Finally, in October 1980, President Jimmy Carter signed the Mental Health Systems Act, which funded community mental health centers. Several months later, Ronald Reagan, who was now the president, effectively ended that program. The result: ever-higher numbers of mentally ill patients, often homeless, roamed American streets, often committing crimes, being incarcerated in prisons that did not provide any treatment, and, over and over again, creating difficult problems for police officers.

When police officers responded to a Signal 27, it typically meant they would be dealing with a mentally ill person. Knowing this, the police officers understood that their options were usually limited. There was the possibility of a threat to the individual, others, or property. While it was correct to assess whether these individuals were breaking the law, it was unacceptable to me that the solution was to arrest and jail them. Their actions, albeit often threatening, were fueled by some sort of mental instability. This meant they were often not able to control their behavior, and throwing them in a cage or box would only exacerbate their unhealthy state of mind.

Once I became sheriff, I felt strongly about finding a solution, I sought to identify programs I could model or use as a framework for my police force. I wanted to build a solid team of experts who understood mental illness, law enforcement, and inmate management. The goal was to identify options that would lead to effective de-escalation of conflicts with mentally ill individuals, create sufficient support programs to house and manage them in prison facilities in the event they needed to be put in jail, and develop a training program designed to teach, educate, and equip officers on handling such matters. We sent the director of corrections in the sheriff's office and Pat Hogan, a mental illness expert, out to Memphis, Tennessee, to observe a program that took an approach to humanely handling individuals with mental health issues. Based on their feedback and observations, we created the Crisis Intervention Team (CIT). Initially, we had a small team of officers who volunteered to be a part of the CIT; however, after time, we realized the benefit of the training and mandated it for all officers.

Mentally afflicted people need treatment, not jail (unless they have committed a crime). Like anything new, the program had its struggles, but while I was sheriff, it changed the approach to how officers handled these individuals. This was important to me, and I committed myself to making a difference in the treatment of mentally ill people.

CHAPTER 6

LIFE ON THE STREET: HARD LESSONS LEARNED

The crowd applauded.

I had made it. I had graduated from the police academy and made it through probation.

That's four for four. High school. College. Police academy. Employment-related probation. A guy named Nat Glover, raised in the ghetto by parents undeterred by their own lack of formal education, himself undeterred by the odds stacked against a Black kid in the Deep South, now held three diplomas and was wearing a badge and had been assigned a patrol car. I felt so proud of what I had accomplished and so grateful for all the people who had opened doors for me. All the failures, challenges, and redemptive experiences I had come through had led me to this moment. I was the kid who had survived pneumonia and Ax

Handle Saturday. I wasn't supposed to be here, but here I was. I had never been closer to achieving my goal of becoming a detective.

It was early 1967, only seventeen years after the first Black officers had been added to the Jacksonville Police Department. As I've mentioned, segregation had been fully in force when those pioneers joined the department, compelling those Black men to attend a separate training program and requiring them to report solely to white supervisors. They were prohibited from arresting white suspects and restricted to walking beats rather than riding in patrol cars. It wasn't until 1955 that Black officers were given patrol cars (and only two vehicles at that). It wasn't until 1958 that Black officers were allowed to rise to supervisory positions, though with only Black officers under their command. And it wasn't until 1966—the year I entered the Jacksonville Police Department—that the force was at least partially integrated.

As you know by now, when I applied for the police force, my ultimate goal was to become a detective. But no male officer could begin his career in the detective division (though back then, women could because female officers were not permitted to patrol in uniform). Male officers had to start on the street, in uniform, and earn elevation to detective status. And so I did—and I didn't mind that at all. In many ways, I consider being a street officer one of the main highlights of my career. I was fortunate that I was able to ride in a patrol car. In fact, I was among the first Jacksonville police officers to ride in integrated patrol cars. In response to complaints in the late 1960s, when the force still wasn't truly integrated, management selected six officers—three white and three Black—to ride as integrated teams. I really enjoyed patrol duty, maybe due to my approach to life, which was not to take many things quite as seriously as my partners.

One day my partner and I were following up on an arrest warrant when we were directed to the location of the potential suspect. As we exited our vehicle in front of the house where our suspect was sitting, he noticed us and immediately took off running. Naturally, we took off after him. Younger than my more experienced partner and just a few years beyond playing college football, I caught the suspect and handcuffed him. My partner resented the young man for running. Because some young men believed the notion that they could outrun the police or wouldn't be pursued, it was no surprise that he also believed he could outrun us. But we pursued and apprehended him. He was stunned that I was able to catch him. Nonetheless, this is where things nearly took a turn for the worse.

My partner, huffing and puffing, caught up with us. He was miffed, to say the least. He began jostling the suspect, pulling, pushing, and yanking him around. He screamed, "Why did you make us chase you? Why did you make us run?" He was ready to take matters into his own hands, and I knew that I couldn't—I wouldn't—let him manhandle the guy. I pushed my partner away and told him to calm down. Although he never mentioned it, I believe he soon appreciated my intervention.

We were going to put the suspect in jail. It was not the first time, nor the last time that I was caught between my duty and instinct as a police officer and my moral compass. The desire to support your partner is a cultural benefit and issue for police officers. Yes, as partners, we should and must have each other's back; it's crucial to our survival while patrolling the streets. However, it can become detrimental when you have a partner who decides to cross moral and ethical lines. Doing what's right and adhering to cultural norms is sometimes a delicate balance for officers.

Back then, and even today, if you pulled a partner off a suspect or otherwise intervened in that kind of altercation, your partner may have told other officers that you were "soft." This was another way of saying that you were not a team player and could not be trusted to maintain the unspoken code that "we watch each other's back." But when I pushed my partner away from the suspect, I felt like I was watching his back. Police officers believe that they must look out for one another, even if one of us crosses the line. Many don't report other officers to upper management or inform on them in any other way. This can go so far as to tolerate the "throw down," illegally planting a gun or knife by an officer on a crime scene, which is meant to justify beating or shooting an unarmed suspect.

Too often, even today, even with heightened public scrutiny through social media channels, the prevailing code among police remains the same: we have to protect one another, no matter what. But this must change. Sure, this code solidifies the trust between police officers, but ultimately, it undermines public trust and the integrity of the badge.

I recall when Jerry Spates and I patrolled a stretch of Ashley Street near downtown Jacksonville. At the time, this was a busy commercial center for the Black community, dotted with bars, clubs, movie theaters, and so on. It was also a popular rendezvous point for prostitutes, their customers, and a variety of scam artists. On this day, we saw a prostitute walking down the street arm in arm with a guy we knew was not her husband or boyfriend.

We were certain that we were witnessing the start of a scam in action, which would work like this: The prostitute would take her john to a place to, let's say, complete the transaction. Suddenly, her pimp would burst in, accuse the guy of having sex with his wife, draw a gun, and then rob the guy blind. The victim would not be inclined to report the robbery to police, given that the circumstances could arouse uncomfortable questions from the john's wife, girlfriend, or whomever.

Jerry decided to take the lead on this one. "What's going on here?" he asked the couple. "Oh," the guy said sincerely, "I'm just walking down the street with my fiancée." Jerry was perplexed as to how this guy, who revealed to us that he was in the navy, could have been convinced that this woman was actually his fiancée. It became obvious to us that they must have had prior dealings and time spent together. We had seen many schemes before, but this one seemed quite more involved than usual. Nonetheless, this instance touched Jerry's nerve in a way it hadn't in the past. At the time, I felt he overreacted, which tickled me; I couldn't quite suppress my laughter at his reaction. Jerry, on the other hand, immediately became aggravated. He saw no humor in this.

In a deep, serious voice, Jerry said, somewhat ungenerously, "Fiancée? Fiancée? She is nothing but a whore."

To which the woman responded in a soft and humble tone: "Well, a person can change."

"What are you talking about?" Jerry responded. "You were whoring just last night."

We were fortunate to intervene before the man could be robbed and before the woman was defiled, likely keeping them both out of a world of trouble. For the record, let me state that I do not think prostitution is a funny matter, and I acknowledge that the way law enforcement viewed and talked about prostituted women back then is not acceptable today.

Jerry never got over that episode, and I never really let him. For thirty-five years, this was one situation neither of us would ever forget. Unfortunately, Jerry suffered a stroke in August 2013 and died in the hospital. He was sixty-nine years old and had served on the police force for nearly thirty years, ultimately becoming its first Black chief of detectives and the first black director of corrections; he became one of my aides when I rose to sheriff. A 1977 graduate of Edwards Waters College, Jerry now has a building on campus named after him. He was a fine officer and a terrific friend. I visited him in the hospital the day before he died, and we still were grinning over that "person can change" remark. I miss him dearly.

Needless to say, we were not always laughing out there on the streets. I remember one case in particular that still cuts deeply. It ended with a woman losing her life. On that day, my partner and I answered a domestic violence call involving a couple. The woman said her husband had been beating her. Back then, we were trained to find a way to neutralize situations like that without taking someone to jail. We tried on-the-spot counseling (for which we were not fully prepared), threats that stopped short of actual arrest, or anything we could do to reestablish peace. To a large degree, the situation was left to our judgment.

In this case, however, the woman obviously had been badly beaten and was quite frightened. Meanwhile, the man was being verbally aggressive toward her and toward us. She deserved it, he told us. He needed to "straighten her out." Teach her a lesson. I was visibly upset, though my partner seemed to keep his cool. I thought we had enough evidence and cause to arrest the man, but my partner disagreed. He was the senior officer, and I deferred to his judgment. This was an unusual position for us, given that I usually was the team member who looked for a reason not to make the arrest.

My partner thought arresting the man would only make the situation worse. He would go to jail. She would need to bail him out. She would have to testify, which probably would not happen based on our experiences in the past. So we did our best to calm the situation down and left.

When we arrived at work the next day, an officer going off duty asked us if we'd had a call during our last shift at that address. I remembered the address well, as I half expected the need to return there. "I just wanted to let you know," the officer told us, "that the man killed that lady. Shot her six times."

I was shaken, speechless, immensely sad, and regretful. After that shift, I went to the morgue and looked at the woman's body. I told her I was sorry, but I know that my apologies were insufficient. I let her down, and it cost her her life. I'd known that her husband had needed to go to jail. I don't blame my partner because we had been in similar situations before that ended in a better resolution, but this was different.

Today, the law and our guidance are quite different. If any evidence of battery exists, officers are required to arrest the apparent perpetrator. But still, I cannot forget that woman, and I carry the weight of that incident to this day. I failed her.

I soon investigated a similar situation where a man beat his wife. My partner did not want me to arrest the guy, but I couldn't stop thinking of what had happened the last time. So I told the suspect to step out onto a screened-in porch—just him and me.

I told him, "If you hit her again and we get a call back here, I'm going to shoot you somewhere in a place that really hurts. I will tell the people downtown that you tried to take my gun, and I had to shoot you." He replied, "You can't do that." I responded, "I can, and I will."

Unconventional? For sure. Overstepping my authority? Almost certainly. I also have to admit that this was not one of my finest hours as a law enforcement officer. And I can also add that someone could make the case that it tarnished the badge. But I did not want to have to take another trip to the morgue and apologize under those circumstances. We never did have to return to that house.

And then, there was the burning house incident—one that could have proved fatal to me but ended up bringing me to the attention of the public and my departmental superiors. Responding to a house fire call, Jerry Spates and I found the home fully engulfed by flames and a woman standing out front, desperate for assistance. "He's still in there!" she screamed. "He's still in there!"

We went around the back of the house and broke open the back door. I saw the man on the kitchen floor, flames billowing just a few feet above him. At that point, I knew what I had to do. I understood that if I didn't do it, I would find it difficult to live with the guilt forever. I couldn't let this man die. I crawled over the back porch and into the kitchen. Snaking under those flames, I grabbed his arm and pulled him out of the house and into the backyard. The last thing I remember is my partner saying, "Hold on. Hold on. We'll get you there."

I awakened in the hospital, where I had been treated for smoke inhalation. Fortunately, I quickly recovered, and they released me that night. This incident was cited later in my Officer of the Year designation and was remembered by many in the department. Sometimes you have to run toward the fire, not away from it.

I recall another situation that stays with me to this day. A woman had called the police to inform them that children were walking through her yard. Go take a look, I was told. OK, sure. How bad could this be? You just never know.

I was in a one-man squad car, with backup a few minutes behind me. When I arrived, the woman stood in her yard on the walkway between her house and her gate. I had learned to quickly assess a situation as I arrived at a scene. I immediately realized that she was the complainant and, by her body language, agitated. I got out of the car and opened the gate to walk up to her. Then I realized I had not fully assessed the situation. She raised a .45-caliber revolver and pointed it at me. I knew that this weapon could be fired too easily and even unintentionally. When she pointed that weapon at me, the barrel of the gun looked large enough for me to crawl up in. She kept saying she was tired of them, tired of the kids from Eugene Butler Middle School, just down the road.

"They're ruining my yard," she said. "They're ruining my yard." She was distraught and did not seem fully aware of her surroundings or circumstances. The gun was still pointed at me. Her hands were shaking. She was crying. I wasn't worried about her shooting me intentionally; I was very worried about her shooting me unintentionally. Either way, I'd be shot. Others also were worried. Another officer drove up, saw what was happening, and immediately radioed a Signal 34. *Officer needs help.*

I kept quietly saying, "Ma'am, I am here to help you. I am on your side." I never raised my voice above a whisper. I slowly walked up to her, lightly grabbed the cylinder of the gun, and since the hammer was not cocked back, I felt relieved and safe as I slowly moved the weapon away from my direction and told her to let it go. She did. I defused the situation and arrested her.

The words my training officer said to me all those years ago still echo in my head today: "Glover, what you say and how you say it matter."

What he taught me made a difference then and now. It likely saved my life and the lives of others because it was a technique I employed time and again. It became especially useful when I became a hostage negotiator during a later phase of my police career—another high-risk position, though one that tiptoed between drama and comedy.

Once again, I was in a single-unit patrol car when I received a call about a disturbance. It was customary for at least two officers to respond to such calls, so even though I was the lead on this one, I waited around the corner from where the incident had happened for my backup to arrive before responding. My backup didn't show for whatever reason, so I decided to drive to the corner and evaluate the situation. Someone saw me, and one of the people on the scene yelled, "The police have arrived!" I couldn't retreat now, so I drove my car to the edge of where the crowd stood and assessed the situation.

A woman, clearly the victim, was crying. And a man, clearly the apparent abuser, was pacing around in the crowd. "I don't care about the police!" he shouted. "I am not going to jail!"

I walked over to the woman, spoke with her for a bit, and determined that she had been hit. Trying to stall until my backup arrived, I asked a few more questions but ran out of time. If I had asked more questions, it might appear obvious that I was stalling. The abusive man kept inflaming the situation, so I engaged him verbally but in hushed tones to avoid exacerbating the problem, and I put him in a position in which he felt he had to preserve his pride in front of the crowd.

"Yes, I hit her!" he shouted. "I was trying to knock her head off." In a controlled voice, scarcely above a whisper, I told him he was under arrest. He again screamed, more at the crowd than at me, "Didn't you hear me? I am not going to jail! Are you deaf or something?"

I spoke directly to him in a low tone so no one could hear what I was saying. My intention was to de-escalate things so that he wouldn't be compelled to respond aggressively and act on his comments to the onlooking crowd. "I need you to walk over to the car so I can search you." Determined to make a scene and appease the audience of spectators, he barked, "I am not going to jail!"

I again calmly told him that if he did not get into the car, I would radio for additional officers. As the man was still noncompliant, I nonchalantly repeated, a bit firmer this time, "If you continue not to comply, I will be forced to summon even more officers." I waited for him to process the enormity of my words, however exaggerated they may have been.

By now, an even larger crowd was building around us. The situation began to quickly escalate into a more serious event. I whispered to him that I would continue to call for as many officers as it would take to put him in the car. I leaned in, close to his ear, ensuring that the crowd could not hear me, and said through gritted teeth, "Once the other officers get here, and we get you in that car, our first stop will be the hospital before we take you to jail."

He lowered his voice. "Wait a minute," he said. "How did the hospital get into the conversation?" He looked at my face and read between the lines, realizing what I had implied. He now understood that he had one choice in the matter. Under my direction, he walked over to the police car and placed his hands on the roof. I searched him and placed him in the back seat. The crowd applauded. At about that time, my backup unit finally showed up, but it was all over. Sometimes backup officers are intentionally late in responding due to adverse relationships or any number of other circumstances. I had and still have no reason to believe that was the case in this situation. But the larger lesson I learned was that staying calm allowed me to defuse the situation with no additional harm to anyone.

CHAPTER 7

AMBITION ACHIEVED: BECOMING A DETECTIVE— AND MORE

They asked if I had a death wish.

I t wasn't enough.

As satisfying as the work as a patrol officer might have been, my original and overriding ambition still had not been fulfilled. I had successfully navigated probation and service as a street cop, but I still was not a detective—or, in the official parlance of the department at that time, an "investigator."

I remember praying to and pleading with God. If He would allow me to be a detective in the Jacksonville Police Department, I would never ask for anything again because He would have fulfilled my dream. Not many such slots were available, and I was told that my wait would be long. But I thought I had an edge: that college degree.

That, apparently, was the key. Or maybe just one key. Regardless, after just three years on the force and about two years on the street, I received word in 1969 that I had been selected. My dream was realized. *Detective* Nat Glover. I was here! I had achieved my life's dream. This accomplishment came earlier than anyone, even me, had thought it would. However, I knew in my soul that this was God's divine timing, and He knew I was ready. At the age of twenty-six, I was one of the youngest officers on the force. I was also one of the youngest detectives and one of only two Black detectives.

My wife believed I could do anything. She was my biggest supporter. However, even she questioned the timing of things. She admittedly wondered, "Isn't this kind of quick?" But despite it all, she always knew I would make it to this destination.

It was now my time to trade the beat cop uniform for a professional suit. I had already been influenced and encouraged to dress sharp and keep manicured nails by a riding partner of mine. He often warned me to be mindful of my appearance because we never know what people are looking at. Additionally, the more put together I was, the more influence, access, and opportunities I'd get. I opted to treat myself and purchased two moderately expensive suits and five sports jackets. I wanted to look the part as much as I yearned to be the part.

I hoped to join the homicide squad, which is a high-profile position, but I was assigned instead to burglary and later to robbery, which can be more dangerous. With homicides, you usually deal with a one-time incident, an act of passion, or a targeted hit. With robberies, you're usually dealing with serial offenders, people who have been exhibiting antisocial and violent behavior over a period of time and don't mind committing violence again, especially to remain free. Assigned to the burglary unit, I wasted little time in recommending that my friend and frequent patrol partner, Jerry Spates, also be elevated. He was. Things were changing. Slowly, to be sure, but also quite evidently.

As a detective, I initially investigated burglaries and later worked in the General Detail Unit investigating flimflam swindlers and forgeries, which included writing bad checks. At that time, the burglary unit was the entry point for most rookies in the detective division. Solving burglaries and other forms of offenses—in other words, identifying and arresting suspects—was difficult because you typically didn't have much evidence. I remember we turned one case into multiple cases that we cleared by driving a cooperating suspect around some neighborhoods as he helpfully pointed out some of the houses he and his team had burglarized. That was nice, but it was pretty rare. In order for me to solve more cases, I would need to develop a more sophisticated skill set.

Later, as a sergeant in the detective division, I was fortunate to have attended hostage negotiation school, and that training greatly impacted my career. It distinguished me from my peers, and it brought me unsolicited public attention. It taught me important interpersonal skills.

The captain had ordered one of our lieutenants in the investigation division to identify a volunteer to attend hostage negotiation school because its need had become apparent due to a sharp increase in bank robberies throughout the nation. The robbers were often caught inside the banks, which required negotiations because there were hostages involved. They obviously wanted a sergeant, but no one else wanted to go, so I volunteered. My colleagues teased me from time to time about this. No extra pay raise, they said, no additional time off, no hazard premium. All of that was true, but I didn't care. They asked if I had a death wish. Of course I didn't, though I often found myself negotiating with armed individuals who were constantly threatening to commit suicide or inflict mayhem on others.

One of the most noteworthy cases occurred on April 3, 1977, when a Greyhound bus carrying thirty-eight passengers ended up in Jacksonville after being hijacked in nearby St. Augustine by a fellow who was overly fond of alcohol. The SWAT team shot out its tires, and an FBI agent and I began negotiating with the hijacker, twenty-eight-year-old Ronnie Nance, who was drunk and despondent over a recent separation from his wife. In the end, he was subdued on the bus, and no one was hurt.

Asked by reporters why he hijacked the bus, putting those passengers, the driver, and himself in danger, Mr. Nance responded: "I had nothing better to do—seriously." The newspaper story included my name, elevating my profile within the department and in the wider community. (Most people who didn't know me were surprised to learn that I was Black.)

The day after that case broke, I received a letter of commendation from Sheriff Dale Carson. "You displayed great skill as a negotiator and showed courage in your actions by meeting face-to-face with this armed man and successfully bringing this incident to a conclusion without personal injuries to anyone," the sheriff wrote. "Your actions displayed your ability to put into use your training, and you are truly a credit to this department."

This was a major landmark of my ascension within the department. After that incident, it seemed like every person in the sheriff's department wanted to know about this person named Nathaniel Glover.

One winter night, I received a call for another situation that required delicate negotiations. I was on my way to the grocery store, so I was not dressed for anything more than getting out of the car, going into the store, and getting back into the car. When the call came, I entertained thoughts about going back home to get a warmer jacket, but I decided to go directly to the incident. When I arrived at the scene, on one of the local bridges here in Jacksonville, I learned that a man had climbed up the support rails above the bridge and was threatening to jump off into the water.

Standing on the bridge while getting a briefing on the situation, I was so cold that I could hardly concentrate. After the briefing, I climbed up the support rails and began talking to the subject. It seemed even colder up there, and the frigid wind felt like it was blowing through me. After about thirty minutes of discussion, the man indicated that he needed to end everything and just jump. For about ten seconds, I found myself hoping it would end that way as well. But I caught myself and intensified my plea for him to come down. He eventually relented, came down, and gave up. I was so glad he did not jump. If he had, I always would have wondered if the tenor of my negotiations, affected by me being cold and miserable, had changed enough to cause him to jump and commit suicide. I knew I wouldn't have been able to live with his suicide if I had been a factor in not preventing it.

Luckily, we both survived. Experience taught me to show empathy, but the more exact motivators were my commitment to never run away from a tough situation and to maintain my perfect record of never losing a suspect with whom I negotiated.

CHAPTER 8

ONWARD AND UPWARD: RISING THROUGH WHITE RANKS

A career is not made in a day.

Itook the oath as one of Jacksonville's Black police officers in 1966, and I was elected Jacksonville / Duval County's first Black sheriff almost thirty years later, in 1995. What happened in between at the Jacksonville Sheriff's Office (JSO)? So much happened that, looking back, it seems like a blur.

But as is the case for everyone who is sufficiently fortunate to enjoy a long career, if I rerun these memories in slow motion, I can discern key moments and critical lessons—not merely for myself but, more significantly, for my community, for my nation, and for my race.

In the mid-1960s and 1970s, there was a conscious, deliberate effort to integrate the police force. But like any change, there was some opposition, noticeable in the systematic foot-dragging by opposers in decision-making positions. Black officers had faced many trials and slights but were ready for change. We advocated and found strategic opportunities to work across racial lines to promote change, integration, and collaboration. While many white people pushed back on initiatives for change, there were people such as Mayor Lou Ritter and other powerful, influential, fair-minded white people who responded to societal evolutions and to their own best impulses. Change was in the air.

Upon starting with the Jacksonville Police Department, I was befriended by some of the Black officers on the force. They were kind and had good intentions of showing me the ropes. While the majority of Black officers served with integrity and honor, there were some who told me not to make any waves, to stay under the radar for my twenty years on the force, and just plan for retirement.

But quietly serving my twenty years and then collecting my pension checks were not enough for me. I wanted to do more. I wanted to do what the white officers were doing. I wanted to be in charge, to be a decision-maker, a leader, and one in authority. It was not my desire simply to be a follower; I had dreams for something much more important and impactful than that. I wanted to be in a position where I could use my judgment and decision-making skills to extend grace, understanding, empathy, and leniency by opening doors of opportunity for those who may have otherwise been looked over due to past trivial situations, lack of exposure (or what some may call being well-rounded), or simply coming from the wrong side of the tracks. I wanted to do for others what had been done for me.

When I was hired, the department was dominated by white bosses. Everything important in the department was the responsibility of white male officers. They were telling everyone where to go, when to go, who goes, and who stays. They had so much power and control. I wanted to do what they were doing.

I remember telling someone one day that I wanted to do what they were doing, and their response was, "Yeah, right, Glover." They brushed me off. But I wanted to do something significant, and I did not want to just cruise to retirement.

I had been motivated to become a detective, not a chief or ranking officer over detectives. I wanted to be an impactful detective who influenced the decision-making around the consequences or outcomes of those who passed through the criminal justice system.

As a detective, I wanted to find a way to distinguish myself. I went above and beyond my call of duty. I worked weekends and overtime and took on extra cases. I wanted to create and demonstrate a mentality and zeal that would separate me from my peers.

As a patrol officer, I listened to all the people I thought were good officers, and they shared their hard-learned tips with me. I rode with one officer who frequently talked about the importance of attire. He was always carefully groomed and sharply dressed from head-to-toe. His words were what inspired and influenced my style when I became a detective. He is why I believe quality is more important than quantity. Whether consciously or not, I believe that my well-put-together appearance enabled me to be regularly selected for prominent assignments.

I had begun to separate myself from the rest. My work ethic, along with my style and flair, often led my boss to choose me as his stand-in whenever he could not attend a meeting or make an appearance. My peers would often ask me why the boss had selected me to represent him. I would simply say, "I don't know," although I suspected it was because of my appearance, which may have given me a more professional edge.

When I was elevated to the rank of detective sergeant, I remember Lieutenant Nicholson acknowledging my efforts and telling me that I was "head and shoulders" above my peers. This led to razzing from some of my peers, who derisively nicknamed me "Head and Shoulders." But it was a good thing. Nicholson meant it as a compliment, and I took it that way.

I spent a lot of time observing Nicholson and other supervisors. Some were lackluster and uninspiring. Some just cruised and coasted. But others, like Nicholson, really differentiated themselves through their ability to motivate, inspire, and encourage their teams. My leadership philosophy is based on the different styles of leadership I observed when I was in the police academy, when I was an officer, and when I was a detective.

I was encouraged and wanted to model the motivating behaviors I observed. In order to advance in my career, I began reading about leadership and found the books I read to be very informative. I started researching and accumulating considerable knowledge on the topic. I wanted to apply proper leadership skills in a way that made a difference.

And so, in 1974, after five years as a detective, I was offered an opportunity to become a police sergeant. I passed the test and gained that promotion. I was not sent back to the street to train as a patrol sergeant; instead, in an unusual and possibly unprecedented move, the hierarchy kept me in the detective division.

Looking back, I think that the hierarchy had decided that, given my previous performance and growing public presence, I could be the person to help them shatter some racial stereotypes still pervasive within the department. So now I was Detective Sergeant Nat Glover, and I soon was in charge of a burglary squad that, aside from one other African American, was entirely white. It is here that our squad truly made its mark. We had the highest case-solving rate out of all other burglary units in the sheriff's department.

My diligence in honing my leadership skills certainly came in handy now, as I had a team of officers reporting directly to me. Most of my work as a supervising detective was administrative, and I did not personally close a lot of cases. I led my team with clarity, integrity, and fairness.

I tried my hardest to learn from the negative and positive reinforcement I received in the force and offer my unit leadership that both challenged and honored them. I respected my team, and they reciprocated. I knew that the position I held was unprecedented, and I employed every leadership skill I had learned to manage well.

I was the first person of color to have the position of detective sergeant, which included a supervisory responsibility. I had a squad of seven detectives who, of course, gave me the opportunities to shine. I made it clear that I would pay attention to every facet of what they were supposed to be doing and hold them accountable for their work. I was also fortunate to have had extensive experience in the area of investigating burglary cases. And I made certain that they knew that. I further made it clear that I would be looking at the clearance rates on an individual basis, and I would also be sensitive to what we were doing as a team. I also wanted to send a message that under no circumstances would I be satisfied with mediocrity in individuals or on the team. The cases assigned to me and my team were generally in a certain area of town, and I wanted us to distinguish ourselves in that area, which we could do.

It was also clear to me that my team would take my lead. So I demonstrated a level of energy that I wanted them also to exhibit. I was willing to come in early and work late without hesitation or reservation. I wanted to be a role model for them. I also made certain they knew that I was not just signing their investigation reports without carefully reading them. I wanted them to know that I was following their cases by consistently asking them specific questions about those cases. I realized that other detective supervisors sometimes signed off on their subordinates' investigations without reading their reports. I guess one could make the case that they trusted their subordinates. But I wanted to set the tone with my detectives that I read every word and every detail of their reports. And when I had a compliment, I made certain that others heard it; conversely, when I had complaints or criticism, I voiced those in private.

It paid off for my team and me. I was recognized by the Sheriff's Office and several other organizations as Police Officer of the Year because of the work that my talented team had done. On his speaking circuit, the sheriff was commending our accomplishments by stating that we were clearing burglary cases at a rate three times the national average. And the accolades kept coming.

The sheriff further stated that burglary cases were among the most difficult to solve because so little evidence was available at the crime scene. But through hard work and persistence, we closed cases at significantly higher rates than other teams. We managed to consistently top the national clearance rate of 18 percent.

As I navigated my rise through the ranks, I was blessed with the support of many of my superior officers—men who ignored or overcame the prejudicial impulses of some around them. It was with their help that I became more than a tolerated presence—a decorative ribbon—in the department. Word began spreading that I was under consideration for one of the police chief positions.

Sometime earlier, under pressure from Black and other minority leaders, the sheriff began searching for a way to add a Black officer to his upper management team. He didn't want to replace any of his senior white officers because he understood the ramifications of such a move—after all, we were still in the Deep South. However, he also understood the consequences of not identifying a way to incorporate a senior Black officer. The sheriff, I believe, was open to the idea and had a mind for change. But he had to think like a chess player to ensure that both sides, Black and white, didn't feel slighted or edged out. His goal was to try to find balance. So he solved his dilemma by creating a new position. I thought the move was strategically brilliant.

The new position was titled chief of community relations. Though the quiet part wasn't said aloud in public, it was clear that this was a position created for, and to be held by, a Black officer. Some people thought, *Oh, another token position.* But it was a real position and a significant representation of someone who looked like me sitting at a table where the power decisions were made, and many of us were happy about it. We now had, at least in theory, a louder voice and a foothold on real power inside the force.

During the next few years, we saw a succession of African American chiefs of community relations. The first had been Chief Charles Scrivens, and the second was Chief Henry Edwards. The third was ... well, the word on the street was that it would be me.

It was 1985, and I was said to be the leading candidate within the department. Even the Jacksonville *Times-Union* printed something between a rumor and a prediction that I was the heir apparent. The morning when the selection was to be made, I awakened in a deep state of expectation. My wife, Doris, and the kids were primed for a congratulatory celebration that night. I donned my Sunday best. I went to work, awaiting the call to visit the sheriff in his office. The call came, and I went up there.

But I didn't get the job.

Sheriff Dale Carson said: "We've decided at this time that we're not going to bring you on the leadership team."

I have to admit that I slipped into a state of shock. He said something about the great job I was doing, and he said some other nice things, but I honestly couldn't remember them, even five minutes later. I was stunned. It was not the sheriff's protocol to call someone into his office unless he was going to offer you a position. Everyone who thought I would be appointed—my peers, my wife, my family, my friends—rushed through my mind. I just wanted the ground to open up and swallow me.

Now I had to go downstairs and, head held as high as possible, tell everyone it hadn't happened. And, of course, I had to endure a period of time in the department during which I was referred to as "almost" a chief. That reminded me that there were those in the agency who were sympathetic and that there were also those who didn't pass up an opportunity to remind me of my misfortune.

There were several consolations, however: one short-term and one long-term. The short-term consolation was that Jerry Spates—my childhood friend, Black former patrol partner, and buddy—received the promotion. If I couldn't have it, I could not have been more pleased that he had received it. But as close as I was to Jerry and how truly proud I was of him, I had been superior in rank to him, and being passed over like that traumatized me a bit and thrust me into a week of something close to mourning.

When I recovered, and I did rather quickly, the long-term consolation is I made up my mind that the next time an opportunity like that came up, I would make it even more difficult for them to choose someone other than me. In addition, I wanted to know why I had been passed over. Before long, one of my former academy officers said, "You know, Nat, I don't think you'll ever be satisfied until you find out what happened. You need to know this, so I suggest you go up and speak with the undersheriff."

I admit it had crossed my mind that I hadn't been promoted because of my boldness to address specific topics with the undersheriff during a meeting held by the Brotherhood of Police Officers. I was a spokesman for the Blacks in the department, serving in the leadership role for the Brotherhood of Police Officers, which represented Black and other minority officers. The undersheriff had attended one of our meetings so he could hear our concerns. Everyone else decided to remain mute initially, leaving it up to me to tell him, among other things, "We want the use of the N-word to stop." There had been too many meetings where the use of this derogatory word was said openly and freely whenever

Black officers were not in the room. It was shameful how leisurely some of our white colleagues used the word, and no one thought to stop it. Nonetheless, a few white officers in those meetings felt compelled to share this information with me. Now, some may wonder why didn't they speak up in those meetings Again, my best explanation is, this was the Deep South.

The undersheriff seemed receptive to our concerns regarding this matter. He maintained a professional demeanor but didn't go much further with any significant follow-up steps to address it. I also noted, within the department and in a public setting, that some women and Black people were not receiving the promotions they had earned, nor were they being appointed to specialized training programs or sitting on any committees. The most significant thing about the undersheriff's visit to our meeting was that his willingness to simply hear us out gave way for other officers to become open and honest about what they thought and felt. This dialogue paved the way for many future candid discussions with the sheriff and undersheriff, squashing my thought that this was perhaps the reason I hadn't been promoted. So, wanting to understand his decision and through some urging from one of my fellow colleagues, I decided to talk to the undersheriff. He was oblivious to the fact that it bothered me that I hadn't gotten the promotion. However, his demeanor showed that he obviously still thought highly of me. He knew exactly why I was there and appeared pleased that I had come to talk to him.

I asked, "Did I do something wrong? Something I shouldn't have done? Or maybe something I should have done?"

"Glover, don't you know?" he said.

"No, I don't," I responded, somewhat puzzled.

"Glover, you didn't want that position," he said blatantly.

I thought to myself, *Yeah, I did. It would at least double my salary.*

Then the undersheriff said, "Don't you know you're better than that?"

This set me back a bit. *What did that mean?* I thought. I couldn't ask and didn't even want to think about it too much. *Was he saying that the chief of community relations was truly a token position, one that had gone to one of my best friends? Best not to dwell on that,* I thought. But I had gotten what I came for—assurance that I hadn't done anything that caused this apparent setback in my career. I redoubled my efforts to ensure that it wouldn't happen again.

Then one day, about a year later, word came back down to me. The undersheriff wanted to see me again. My colleagues said, "What have you done now?"

When I walked into the undersheriff's office, he was sitting at a conference table with the director of police service. That director, James McMillan, had been a classmate of mine at the academy and later became sheriff. When I sat down, I tried not to look surprised that I had been summoned to this meeting. I said in the most professional tone I could muster, "Undersheriff, Director, how may I help?"

Undersheriff Nelson looked at McMillan and said, "See, that's what I like about him."

Then both men looked at me, and Undersheriff Nelson happily said, "We are going to promote you and bring you on the leadership team as chief of the division of police services."

What? I thought to myself. *This is a big deal.* The scope of work for the chief of community relations was important and carried with it many responsibilities; however, the chief of the division of police services was next-level. In this role, I would have about 150 people under my leadership and have direct oversight of support operations for all officers. I became the first Black person to serve in this position and the first to serve in any position more significant than the chief of community relations. Before anyone could change their mind, I eagerly answered, "I accept the position."

I had broken through various racial and professional frontiers. They had been saving me for this. I believe that Sheriff Carson wanted to find the most indisputably qualified Black officer to put in that position.

White officers were surprised by the appointment, and they understood the significant implications. This now meant that moving forward, all positions would be open to whites, Blacks, and all minorities. It was another significant promotion for me and, moreover, prepared the way for Black officers to become directors, chiefs, undersheriffs, and, ultimately, sheriffs.

At one point, someone in the department found and posted for all to see the court-sealed mug shot of my arrest so many years earlier as a youth. I made certain I did not overreact in a way that indicated they were successful in getting to me. I didn't tear it down, and I reported it to my senior officer. I learned later that the person who put it up was transferred to a different area or unfavorable shift because of that action. This show of disrespect implied that many—too many—officers and support staff were still not ready for a Black boss.

There were crises. It comes with the territory. As chief of the division of police services, my portfolio included the department's communications center and its one hundred dispatchers and other employees, the records and identification unit, the supply unit (uniforms, radios, weapons, and other equipment), the motor pool and all its vehicles, and the procurement section (though it generally was handled by a deputy director). The dispatchers are particularly key links in the chain of law enforcement. They must properly assess each call, especially the degree of risk it might present to responding officers, and they must clearly relay that information to the officers. The expertise and performance of police dispatchers have life-and-death consequences. And like all other employees, they have personal issues from time to time.

At one point, a female African American dispatcher came to me. She held a doctor's letter stating that she needed to be on a permanent morning shift rather than the usual rotating shifts due to issues regarding her pregnancy. This seemed reasonable to me, so I moved her to the morning shift and told the schedulers not to place her on rotation. Alas, several white dispatchers found this less than reasonable. They went directly to Sheriff McMillan and asserted that I was giving the Black woman favorable treatment solely because she was Black. I happened to be passing the sheriff's office as they were leaving and, distracted by the other matter, didn't give much thought to what I saw.

Later the sheriff called me into his office and relayed their complaint. I responded, "They have not told you the whole story and—"

He interrupted me: "I know you. You don't have to explain, but given what I have planned for you, I need you to go make this right—just fix it."

I was a little upset. But then, I never entertained an attitude, and I do not believe in reprisals. I knew I had not done anything wrong, but I also acknowledged that, at times, feelings are as important as facts. I understood that the white dispatchers believed I was helping the young lady only because she was Black. But they didn't understand that my instinct was to help, and I wanted to help keep her on the job, which I would have done for any one of the white dispatchers in the same situation. Because of my nature and desire to learn a lesson from every situation, I never raised the issue with the other dispatchers, but I did devote special effort to demonstrating my support for the work of all complaining dispatchers and addressing any specific needs they might have. My goal was to effectively demonstrate actions that would mitigate the perception that I was biased. The sheriff felt it was crucial that I fix the situation and ensure there wasn't any ambiguity in my intentions to be fair and equitable.

At another point during this phase of my career, a true tragedy shook the entire department: an officer was shot dead while on duty. He had been wearing a bulletproof vest. And although the bullet had struck several major organs, a subsequent investigation revealed that the bullet had not penetrated his vest. Yet rumors spread that the vests provided by my supply unit were inferior. This simply was not true, but it took some time to sort out, and it led to many tense days and confrontations.

It was a gut-wrenching moment—being compelled to defend the vests and the people who had purchased them while at the same time grieving for a colleague. In the end, I presented the facts, the tension dissipated, and the environment returned to normal, but it certainly was another learning opportunity.

These and other challenges were inevitable, but I tried to learn from them and leverage them as motivation in future endeavors. Just as a football running back shakes off tacklers, I wanted to keep my eye on the goal line and keep moving forward.

Over the next nine years at JSO, I achieved promotions as deputy director of police services and then director of police services. I reported to the undersheriff. In addition to my previous duties, I now oversaw jails and prisons, human resources, maintenance, and basically everything that was nonoperational. My breakthrough had occurred, but there was no room for error. This ascension was challenging and exhilarating. And it was not over.

Becoming a detective was my original destination. However, as I climbed through the ranks of detective, I began to realize that my influence and impact within the force and within the community held significant meaning. Transitioning outside of the detective's unit and subsequently into higher-ranking positions was the catalyst for Black officers to follow their own dreams of rising within the force. But most importantly, I feel that God's divine order was at play once again, and He knew I'd be needed for such times when change was ripe for the season.

The sky was now the limit for us.

CHAPTER 9

RUNNING FOR SHERIFF: I WANTED TO SEE A BURNING BUSH

The Bold New City of the South.

Serving as sheriff, even running for election as sheriff, was not something that I entertained as I was growing up—or at any point during my law enforcement career. The thought was too outlandish to generate even a spark of such ambition. A Black man from the ghetto not only serving a predominantly white county in the Deep South but actually running a law enforcement agency in such a place? Give me a break. Even if the thought had arrived spontaneously, my first thought would have been, *This is unprecedented!* There were no paths to follow, no models to emulate. I would be the pioneer. I would have to blaze the trail. But I also believe in a divine purpose that creates the tools required to reach a destination. In this case, I believe that is what happened.

In early 1994, Sheriff James McMillan, my friend and former class-mate at the police academy, decided he would not seek reelection. He had been appointed in 1986 by Governor Bob Graham to complete the term of retiring sheriff Dale Carson. McMillan had been elected twice to continue as sheriff, and now he was retiring. Soon after, I ran into Pastor John Newman of Mount Calvary Baptist Church. A man of influence who served as a bridge between Black and white communities, he recently had arrived in Jacksonville from Philadelphia, where Black folks had gained some electoral footholds, having elected their first Black mayor.

Pastor Newman felt strongly that I should run to succeed Sheriff McMillan, a thought that really hadn't occurred to me. He said I had positioned myself well, and this was our time. A few other people also suggested that I run for office, but I brushed them off. I had no experience or interest in politics, was not well-known in the community, and saw no way that an African American could win such an election. After all, three white officers already had declared themselves as candidates, and racial divisiveness still defined Jacksonville, with Black groups in court at that very moment suing over lingering segregation in our schools.

Instead, I planned to retire gracefully. I was more than satisfied with my existing accomplishments within the JSO. I just hoped that the department would be blessed with another sheriff as fair and effective as Jim McMillan. If I were going to run, I would need a sign from God. I would need to see my own burning bush. And then I did.

Coming to similar conclusions regarding local racial politics, McMillan endorsed W. C. Brown for sheriff. Asked by reporters on February 3, 1994, why he wasn't endorsing a Black officer, he said, "Whether or not our community has progressed enough to be able to elect a Black, I don't know."

Boom. The bush wasn't just ignited—it exploded. Black residents and many white residents were furious. "Enough," they said. "Enough of this. It's the mid-1990s, and Jacksonville must move into the light." My friend and partner, Jerry Spates, and I huddled and decided that one of us should keep our minds open about running for office. Neither of us wanted the intense scrutiny it would bring, but we decided that I had the best shot at it—and I didn't want the potential guilt of knowing I had been afraid to shoulder the challenge. Suddenly I was on the receiving end of electoral pressure. A diverse collection of community leaders encouraged me to run as a Democrat for sheriff. Their basic rationale: I had achieved more than notable success within the department and was held with high regard among the public—and I should not reject what they saw as the ultimate earned promotion.

Needless to say, they thought my candidacy alone also would qualify as a historic breakthrough for African Americans in Florida, the entire South, and maybe much of the nation. Other colleagues and friends believed such an effort would prove futile, bring nothing but embarrassment upon me and my community, and negate my previous achievements. I still did not know what to do. At that point, Pastor Newman reached out to local attorney Steve Pajcic, a cornerstone of the white political establishment who nearly had been elected Florida's governor, and to Steve's brother, Gary Pajcic, who had served as a prosecutor and with whom I had worked on cases in the past. Pastor Newman asked them if they could support a Black candidate.

Steve and Gary had already given this some thought. Shortly after McMillan made that statement about Jacksonville having a Black sheriff, the local newspaper sponsored a community forum in response to the furor his statement had created. Steve attended that session. His response to the dominant question? There was no predetermined answer, and it all depended on the citizens of Jacksonville and what their leaders were prepared to do.

Speaking with Pastor Newman, Steve was more direct regarding his willingness to support a Black candidate. Yes, he said, if it's the right one. They agreed that I could be that man, and Steve offered to run the campaign without charge if I chose to enter the race.

I called Steve and asked him, "Do you think I should run?" I'll never forget his response: "Nat, I'm not in the business of telling you whether you should run or should not run. But if you run, we'll help you."

That was extremely persuasive, but I also kept hearing the naysayers, who ridiculed the very idea. "Glover," they said, "you are not widely known, you haven't raised a penny for a campaign, two white officers are way ahead of you, and, by the way, this is Jacksonville and you're a Black man. Don't mess up your record of success." I was leaning in that negative direction, looking for every compelling justification to exit the race before I truly had entered it. I thought, *Let's see what my wife, my partner and guide through life, has to say.* So I shared all the pros and cons with Doris, with a bias toward the cons.

I knew that reasons not to run would prove compelling and that Doris would respond with a resounding, "No, don't do this." Instead, she said, "I think you should do it. You should run for sheriff."

That threw me. To be honest, I was disappointed in her response. I tried to talk her out of it, but she remained firm. I also spoke with both of my adult children, who remained strongly supportive of me taking my shot. I realized I had nowhere to hide. I had imagined saying publicly, "In my heart, I am full of regret, but I must put my wife and family first. Therefore, with much sorrow, I will not become a candidate for sheriff." I then imagined applause if I decided not to run, with possibly a huge sigh of community relief and everyone telling me I had made the right decision for our community. Now, I was coming around to running. As I shared earlier, one of my greatest fears in life has been not shouldering an important challenge.

Additionally, part of my decision-making process always has been to visualize the worst-case scenario. If that scenario is tolerable, why not move forward? The worst case here: I would earn very few votes, I would lose the race, and some people would snicker. But more importantly, I would end up retiring, just as I had planned. No big difference. So I reluctantly decided to run for sheriff, but first, I would need to confer with one more trusted colleague and adviser, then-circuit judge Brian Davis of nearby Nassau County. I raised the question of whether to run. His answer was, "Glover, do you remember what you told me?"

This was a reference to a moment four years earlier when Brian, also an African American, asked me if he should leave the safe confines of a prestigious law firm to become, as desired by many in the Black community, chief assistant state attorney and one of our region's top prosecutors and the first Black man or woman to hold that position. At that time, I told him, "From my perspective, you do not have the right to say no to this history-making, monumental position that will serve as an example for the African American kids in this city."

Now Brian looked me in the eye and said, "I am telling you the same thing. From my perspective, you do not have the right to say no to this monumental, historic position for an African American in this city."

(By the way, President Obama nominated Brian to serve as a US district court judge, and Brian took that seat on December 26, 2013. Steve Pajcic and I were on the judicial nominating committee recommending him to the president.)

And so, Brian and I both made history in Jacksonville.

Starting late, with an empty campaign chest and no experience, we moved into campaign mode with Steve and Gary Pajcic, other establishment figures, most of the Black community, and much of the white community in my corner. Steve and Gary managed to raise some money, though we still ended up with half the amount of funds available to another leading candidate. I campaigned on foot through countless neighborhoods, back to something similar to walking patrol beats. We carefully focused our message on controlling crime, which was my sweet spot, rather than on race, which could prove detrimental.

"I will not give up one square inch of this city to the criminal element," I told a crowd that gathered during a peaceful march we organized, as several hundred people of all races held hands.

As I recall, our TV commercials echoed that theme: "When I'm sheriff, I won't just sit behind a desk," I said in one of those commercials. "I'll continue to walk these beats. Because to me, every street in Jacksonville is the sheriff's office."

The tagline of every spot: "Nat Glover for sheriff. A tough cop who's earned the job."

One of those commercials triggered a bit of a crisis. It asserted that I had walked or campaigned in every beat of the city. I had not. Almost all of them, yes. All of them? No. I saw the spot on a Friday, and it was set to begin running on the following Monday. Someone in the meeting said, "If he only has a few more to walk out of more than ninety beats, no one will really know." I responded, "I will know, and that is unacceptable to me."

So my wife and I walked the remaining beats over the weekend, maintaining the integrity of the campaign along with my own personal integrity and peace of mind. As the fifteen-month-long campaign rolled forward, we won important endorsements from the media and other opinion leaders.

Jack Fletcher, a highly regarded professor of education at the University of North Florida, was kind enough to say this about me: "He was not only an outstanding student who excelled in both oral and written presentations but a gentleman who gained admiration and respect from his peers in all class participation. His experiences, dedicated service as a law enforcement officer, coupled with his integrity and sound commitment to justice, make him a notable candidate to represent the leadership role of such a prestigious office."

I also was pleasantly surprised by the level of energy, zeal, and passion devoted to my campaign by members of my church, Saint

Stephen African Methodist Episcopal Church, located near downtown Jacksonville. I probably shouldn't have been surprised. The African Methodist Episcopal movement was born in the early 1800s as a protest against slavery and against discriminatory treatment within and has retained a deep connection to racial equity under God. Consequently, a large number of Saint Stephen's approximately one thousand congregants embraced my campaign, devoting time and effort as if it were a regular job. I hesitate to mention specific members for fear of omitting many people I should mention, but Charlene Hill, who soon would serve as executive director of the Jacksonville Human Rights Commission, along with Pastor Michael Mitchell, led the volunteer church effort.

By contrast, I didn't have very much support from my fellow police officers. Most white officers divided their support between the two remaining white candidates, W. C. Brown and Joe Stelma (the third had dropped out along the way), and many Black officers had some reservations about me. They didn't think I had a chance, and they perceived me as someone who was too serious and focused on climbing the ranks. They didn't feel a connection with me as one of the boys or brothers because I didn't spend much time hanging out or being pals with them. Conversely, they knew my work ethic and integrity well, as they often came to me whenever they had a problem on the job.

As it became more apparent that having a Black person on the ticket was important, Joe Stelma set out to diversify his standing; somewhere along the way, he had chosen my friend, Chief Jerome Spates, as his running mate for undersheriff. I'll admit I was surprised and a bit disappointed. Some people thought I should be angry, but I wasn't. Jerry later explained that from a strategic point of view, we, as African Americans, had two chances of having a person of color in the two top spots in the sheriff's office.

Jerry and Stelma enjoyed comfortable support from most Black police officers, as Jerry was very popular among them. His position in public relations afforded him the opportunity to be in front of them often and connect on a level I hadn't. Still, during this campaign, I was blessed to receive unending support from Black officers such as Chief of Community Affairs Joseph Henry, who was one of the most courageous people I had the honor of working with. He did not hesitate to look people in the eye and tell them what they needed to hear. There was also departmental chaplain David Williams, and Officers Tawana Lee and Willie Jones, all of whom frequently accompanied me on campaign swings dressed in full uniform. I always thought that their support was a great example of loyalty and courage. And I'll never forget the faithful few others who supported me.

Incidentally, Officers Lee and Jones also served as my personal body-guards during the campaign. I often mention that I didn't think I needed bodyguards, but I was surprised by the number of people who told me they went to bed many nights worrying about my safety when I was campaigning. Chaplain Williams was a genius at getting me into almost every church in this city during the fifteen months I campaigned for sheriff.

My opposition attempted a strategic move and delivered a story to the *Times-Union* about my arrest for the high crime of possessing two napkins. Ironically, although the *Times-Union* decided to print the story, they had also endorsed me for sheriff. While the judge had sealed the record of that incident, I still thought it looked bad. Except, it didn't. Most readers concluded that if this is all they could find on this guy, they were fine with voting for me.

Election Day, April 11, 1995, came, and though the polls looked good, we didn't know quite what to expect. We certainly didn't expect our large margin of victory. I won 55 percent of the vote, easily defeating my two white opponents. I, who'd had serious misgivings about running at all, had begun campaigning late in the race, and had empty campaign fund coffers, had won. With the blessing of my wife and family, the support of my faith community, and the generosity of political establishment players, I won. I, the little boy who had been held back in school, had made history. I received 94,653 votes. Brown, also running as a Democrat, received 41,562 votes. Stelma, a Republican, attracted 34,594 votes. I won Black neighborhoods, white neighborhoods, and nearly all neighborhoods.

Steve Pajcic stated, "It was a very strong victory. We had a feeling that something like that was coming, but the margins surprised most people."

My campaign headquarters was the scene of pure ecstasy, the streets nearby filled with celebrants. The next morning, the local newspaper ran a two-word banner headline: "GLOVER WINS," and it added that I "ran away" with the race, becoming the first Black sheriff of a major city in the Deep South since the Reconstruction Era. Civil rights pioneer Rosa Parks called and congratulated me generously. In 1955, she had defied an order to sit in the back of a Montgomery, Alabama, bus, serving a historic role in the civil rights movement and earning the congressional descriptions as "the first lady of civil rights" and "the mother of the freedom movement." And now she was speaking to me as if we were old friends. Congratulations also arrived from several sheriffs around the state, including the sheriff of adjoining St. John's County (St. Augustine) and deeply conservative Bay County (Panama City). Jacksonville mayor Ed Austin said: "You just changed this whole city. We chucked our past. I'm proud of you."

I appreciated that, but maybe it was too generous. We still had a lot of work ahead of us (and we still do). I was happy, of course, but my mind almost immediately switched into management mode. *Who would I select for my cabinet? How would we handle ourselves in these coming days and long term?* My model would come from my predecessors, and Sheriff McMillan proved particularly generous. The day after my historic win, he joined me as I completed the first of my many community walks as sheriff-elect and then sheriff. He visibly and publicly demonstrated his support for and solidarity with me, his one-time police academy class-mate. This and many other kind gestures to come from Sheriff McMillan were priceless actions of support. Even though he initially had endorsed someone else, he remained a terrific friend and trusted adviser during those heady days of my first administration, and he remains so today.

So it was done. My new badge read, "Sheriff Jacksonville Police Department." It also read, "The Bold New City of the South."

Jacksonville had stepped up big-time. It was now up to me to do what I had promised.

CHAPTER 10

WITH A LITTLE HELP FROM MY NEW (WHITE) FRIENDS

It was almost a coronation.

In the book of Genesis, the Bible tells us that Abraham was about to respond to what he believed was direction from God to sacrifice his son on the altar. God then redirected him toward a ram in the bush, which was now the designated sacrifice. This is consistent with my personal belief and philosophy that if you do the right thing for the right reason, as Abraham did by being willing to sacrifice his son, the Lord will bless you with the resources required to accomplish your mission and your destiny. This is how I feel about the introduction to my life of Steve and Gary Pajcic. They are of Croatian descent, which made them rather definitely not Black, but we grew up in adjoining neighborhoods and ended up discovering that we had much in common. They founded the law firm Pajcic & Pajcic in 1974 with the lofty goal of making a difference in their community. Through public service, philanthropic donations, and a commitment to seeking justice for their clients, they certainly have accomplished that.

When I was drafted as a rookie politician into that first campaign for sheriff, Steve and Gary were the answer to my prayers. Steve had served six terms as a prominent Democratic member of the Florida legislature. He ran for governor in 1986, and his brother, Gary, was a big part of that campaign. They had come close, losing to Republican Bob Martinez after Steve's opponent in the Democratic primary, Jim Smith, defected, breaking a promise to Steve by endorsing Martinez.

Now, for me, they became brothers from another mother, and their investment in the campaign was second to none—and I'm not referring solely to money. Their impeccable organizational skills and stellar reputations within the community attracted the human resources required by a genuine campaign. Among other moves, they brought in the prominent national campaign consulting firm of Shrum, Devine & Donilon, led by noted Democratic powerhouse Bob Shrum. Shrum had worked with presidential candidates George McGovern, Al Gore, Ted Kennedy, and John Kerry, and now his firm was working with and for me. Unbelievable!

Their involvement and commitment to the campaign allowed me to transition emotionally from a campaign primarily intended to make a point about race to a campaign that also focused on fighting crime and binding together all of Jacksonville's diverse communities. Without Steve and Gary in my life, I would not have accomplished much of what I discuss in this book. Both believed in their souls that Jacksonville was ready to elect a Black sheriff and that I was that person. With Steve working his magic in other ways, Gary chaired my successful 1995 campaign. Gary was the kind of individual who left you with a "we are pals" kind of feeling. He was a star athlete, particularly at Florida State

University, where his performance as the football team's quarterback is the stuff of legend to this day.

As an attorney, Steve devoted himself to helping those on Jacksonville's lower social rungs, and his winning personality surely aided his performance and record in the courtroom. Gary died of a rare form of viral encephalitis at the age of fifty-eight on August 2, 2006. Without warning, he suffered a seizure four days before his death, and there was nothing that could be done for him. Following his death, Steve and I bonded even more tightly. We had grown up a mile from each other, not far from Edward Waters College. We both had a brother who was a better athlete than we were. We both had married early and married well. And we both had found a friend as close as the brothers we had lost. This is what Steve has to say about all of this:

> Regardless of race, Nat Glover was obviously the most qualified candidate for sheriff and the best for Jacksonville. Rather than making a racial statement, it was even more important that Jacksonville select the best person for the job. Nat didn't really know anything about politics, but he was a great candidate for sheriff and a great speaker. He has some of the preacher in him. Some of the most effective public speakers we ever had in the United States were Black kids from the ghetto. There is no connection in my mind between the position of birth and effectiveness as a public speaker.
>
> And it turned out that Jacksonville and its leadership were ready for a Black sheriff. His election [was so sweeping] that it was almost a coronation. It definitely was a mark of the progress that Jacksonville has made in race relations—and has not made. There's still lots more to be done.
>
> For Nat, what you have to say is that all of this is a tremendous accomplishment. To come from where he came, the urban ghetto, to

rise to the level of being the first African American sheriff in Florida since the Reconstruction Era.

And not only that, but to become a respected and acclaimed sheriff, that's just a tremendous accomplishment for him. Nat's career is a real testament to him as an individual, and it is an apt metaphor for the evolution of our society and race relations.

Steve and Gary also provided me with a philanthropic model that I strive to emulate, including the millions they donated to educational and other causes. I decided to donate four years of my JSO pension—worth about $240,000. The funds were allocated between the Take Stock in Children Fund and the Sheriff Nat Glover Endowment Fund for needy students. Steve called that, in terms of our relative net worth, "even more generous" than anything he and his family had done. I'm not sure about that. Among their other charitable efforts, Steve and his wife, Anne, donated two million dollars to Edward Waters College after I became its president. He began to fashion a program of how the money should be used but said, "Then, I decided that Nat knows better than me, and his trustees know better." So he gave the money unencumbered.

I was stunned by Steve and Anne's generosity and overwhelming confidence in my abilities. But they were not alone. Also prominent in my corner was Martin Garris, who publicly endorsed me and stood by my side as a highly respected white endorser during nearly every campaign event. Martin, an army veteran, spent fifteen years of devoted service in our department, often advocating for Black and other minority officers. Later he served another twenty years as director of police and public safety at the University of North Florida. His work there was so highly regarded that UNF named its police headquarters building for him.

After my election, I brought him back to the department as chief of our Community Affairs Division. He planned to succeed me as sheriff in 2003 but died unexpectedly on September 5, 2002. I miss Martin very much. I'll never forget his devotion to public service, friendship, and loyalty. A life of experiences touched by miracles is living proof that if you do the right thing for the right reasons, the Lord will deliver models and helpers in your life. It is our duty to embrace them, accept them, and learn from them and their example. I reiterate, the Pajcic model compelled me to donate four years of my pension benefits to a college scholarship fund to support needy young people. And it is in their honor that I continue to make charitable donations whenever the opportunity is presented to me.

CHAPTER 11

SHERIFF NAT GLOVER: STEPPING UP TO THE CHALLENGE

**Police officers must be
exceptional, never mediocre.**

After the Civil War, constitutional amendments and the Civil Rights Act of 1866 gave African Americans a semblance of the rights afforded other Americans, including the right to vote. In addition, they were given the opportunity, in some cases, to acquire land that their enslavers had held. This period was known as the Reconstruction Era, though it served as a brief interregnum in the centuries-long oppression of Black Americans.

Opposition to Reconstruction soon flared and, by 1877, triggered the creation of the Ku Klux Klan, renewed suppression of the Black vote, and the initiation of macabre lynchings of thousands of Black men and boys—a campaign of white supremacist terror that persisted for much of the subsequent century.

It was within this history that I took office as the first elected Black sheriff in Florida since the Reconstruction Era, and, moreover, in Jacksonville, a city with an image long tarnished by racial tension little different than that found in the nearby border state of Georgia. So it was no surprise that my election, even in the mid-1990s, made headlines throughout the nation. It was a truly historic breakthrough, a suggestion of change, however slow and hesitant, wavering and insecure.

Hostility didn't magically evaporate. Although I won the race with a diverse representation of voters, it didn't fall flat on me that there was still much work to do. It was as courageous as it was evident that the voters of Jacksonville were ready for something different in government. Not just a new face or a Black face but a different way of governing— and I believe they wanted a dignified way of building bridges. So in no uncertain terms, I unequivocally was determined not to let the citizens of Jacksonville down. My constituency trusted that I was the right person for the job and had the knowledge, skills, temperament, and desire to be effective and lead with integrity. And another important factor, which may not seem to mean much today but was essential back then, is that I was educated. I recall times where voters would call the campaign office and ask, "Is this the one with the master's degree?" Funny as it may sound, it was indeed true. And it contributed to their list of reasons to vote for me.

After I became sheriff, we had an unprecedented number of retirements and other departures. I knew I had my work cut out for me. But God wouldn't have put me in this position if I had not been ready for the challenge. My first act was to reach across the metaphorical aisle and enlist qualified supporters of my opponents as top aides in my administration. In stark political terms, this would be the equivalent of a newly inaugurated US president inviting a member of the opposition party to join their cabinet. I wanted to put the best people I could find in key positions. My approach wasn't initially widely accepted by my team. However, it was important to me because I wanted to send a message that the campaign was over, and it was time to work and bring the department together. I had only one question for the incumbents: "Could you be as loyal to me as you were to my opposition?" If they could answer yes to this question with integrity, they made the roster. This ended up being one of the best decisions I ever made. I was able to select the most qualified people for each position and, at the same time, demonstrate my commitment to serving the entire force and the entire community. No matter how you looked at it, it was a win, and I made certain that I fostered the practice of placing officers where they would excel.

When officers rose to their deserved level of merit, the community benefited from their excellence and devotion. As a leader, I benefited from the enhanced confidence invested in me by my officers and the community, which earned me the benefit of the doubt whenever I had to make tough calls or decisions, which I so often did.

When I took office, I made several changes in the department that I believed were necessary to better serve the community and elevate the rank and file. One of my early policy changes was the academic requirement of candidates. New recruits were now required to have obtained a four-year college degree before joining the force. There were two reasons why this was important. First, it helped to curb the misconduct of officers. Based on feedback from a grand jury investigation, it was determined that the lack of higher education had a direct connection to the misconduct of some officers. Hence, I was tasked with looking at our hiring practices to identify a way to introduce a change in our hiring approach. Second, when you look at the criminal justice system, police and correction officers were the only ones who weren't required to have a postsecondary education. Yet police officers had the lawful power to take a life based on an instant, unilateral decision. It was my belief that with this type of decision-making power, it was critical to have the best person on the streets equipped to do this. Therefore, through higher education, officers would be exposed to the humanities and political and social sciences that would help them become better prepared to make these life-altering decisions and help mitigate some of the biases often associated with determining the best approach to take when dealing with the community. Rest assured; this wasn't just for the rank and file. It applied to new recruits at all levels across the department. In fact, four of the five people in my administration, including myself, all held master's degrees, and the fifth held a bachelor of science in criminal justice.

⚖

During this time, the concept of "community policing" was beginning to gain traction in many parts of the nation. In a nutshell, the term refers to engaging the community in a joint effort with law enforcement to improve mutual understanding and, most importantly, to achieve maximum effectiveness in the policing of that community. Many agencies around the country initiated what they called "community policing programs" but did so in name only, to receive federal grants. We were different. As you will see, we really pressed forward with community policing policies. I truly believed in it.

Several of my initiatives at JSO disturbed many of my officers, but in time, most embraced the changes, and we realized genuine improvement. One of my most controversial actions was ordering that officers' names be stenciled, in stylish cursive, on both sides of their patrol cars, which they were allowed to take home overnight and on their days off. There was no question about the fervor for which we approached community policing. We were undoubtedly going to be a collaborative law enforcement body. We wanted the community to understand that we wanted them to know us as much as we wanted to know them and that we were accountable for our actions. I met with the Fraternal Order of Police (FOP), and we agreed that instead of putting the names on both sides of the car, we'd put them on just one side. Despite the desire to connect with the community and align with the FOP, there was pushback from some of my officers and others.

I received calls from officers' relatives—primarily wives, mothers, and even grandmothers—asking why I was making it so easy for their husbands, sons, and grandsons and those who loved them to become targets for retribution by criminals and troublemakers. They felt their lives could potentially be in danger with this apparent "exposure" of their identity. It was clearly an unpopular policy change for some officers, and some decided to send a clear and symbolic message. One day my city-owned unmarked sedan was vandalized while I was working at police headquarters in downtown Jacksonville. My name had been perfectly stenciled in cursive on a magnet placed on my car while it was parked in the secure lot. The message of rebellion had been made clear to my team and me. The careful nature of the stenciling, performed in a guarded location, meant that this was not the work of a single mutineer. It would have taken at least three officers to watch the building's entrances while one or two performed the deed. This was a group effort—a nice, neat, and professionally done job that was a crime: defacement of public property.

More universally successful was my determination to get more officers on the street and to enhance community policing by creating police substations on every corner of the city. This came partially in response to an explosion of crime, most prominently juvenile violence, in our region and throughout much of the nation. It was said at that time we were losing a generation. I attributed most of this to breakdowns in the home. No ancestral or generational wealth was being passed down, which meant that most parents—both in single-parent and dual-parent households—had to work during the day. The need to take care of the family left gaping holes in managing the household. Children were often left to manage themselves, leaving them susceptible to getting caught up in otherwise preventable situations. Therefore, the substations allowed officers to curb the violence among young people by acting as truant officers. I asked my officers to remain alert throughout the city for truants and when found, these kids were offered (an offer they could not refuse) rides back to school or to an attendance center that we had established in conjunction with the school system. I took particular interest in finding a way to help keep these young people off the street as I recalled my mother telling me that not going to school was not an option. And to this day, I believe that's what saved my life. So I wanted to pay it forward and find a way to keep as many kids as I could off the street, away from juvenile violence, and perhaps save some of their lives.

According to a study by the Urban Institute's Justice Policy Center, the number of juveniles arrested for violent crimes surged by 64 percent between 1980 and 1994. For murder alone, juvenile arrests spiked by 99 percent. It was true: we *were* in danger of losing an entire generation of young people. Dramatic action was required.

During some of my walks around the city, my entourage and I would take a city bus rather than vehicles to the starting point. On one such day, my fully uniformed, medal-bedecked officers and I boarded a bus, and lo and behold, we saw two school-age boys sitting in the back seat. I went back there to question them and sure enough, they were playing hooky. They knew they had blown it. Their eyes were as big as saucers. I told them, "You boys better get back to school right now."

I had campaigned on a promise to assign officers throughout the city, and now it was time to deliver. The department's first plan, under Sheriff McMillan's leadership, was to place substations on the campuses of certain high schools, and we built the first one at Samuel W. Wolfson High School. When I took over, it soon became clear that we lacked the funds to build many more substations, even though I had made that promise. We needed a creative solution, and I found one with the owners of shopping malls. They needed more security, and we needed places to station our officers. Perfect!

Mall owners agreed to contribute, design, and modify appropriate spaces according to our requirements and, importantly, at no cost. With police officers assigned to that zone reporting to duty, the substation presented a police presence that greatly enhanced security at these shopping centers. Soon we had decentralized the sheriff's office, just as I had promised. We established appropriately staffed police substations at four scattered shopping centers and in other sensitive locations around the city, including somewhat later at my alma mater, Edward Waters College.

As a postscript, when I became president of Edward Waters, I led a community effort to raise $1 million, and the sheriff's office contributed $900,000 (of confiscated drug money plus some federal funds) to build the substation on our campus. One of the main programs under my tenure there was a criminal justice program that meshed nicely with the substation that housed many of the program's classes.

Six JSO substations remain open to this day, strategically located at the Gateway Shopping Center, the Regency Square Mall, the Cedar Hills Shopping Center, the Highland Square Shopping Center, near Prominence Parkway, and at Edward Waters University. These are cornerstones of the Jacksonville Sheriff's Office, and I am enormously proud of them.

During my term in office, we built a new state-of-the-art police training academy that included a training pool on the north campus of Florida State College at Jacksonville. We also built an equestrian facility in the downtown area of Jacksonville, which eliminated the need for the mounted unit officers to spend so much time transporting horses to and from the prison farm where the horses were kept that was located in the rural area of Jacksonville. Additionally, we built a state-of-the-art, thirty-eight-thousand-square-foot police athletic building. The $3.6 million structure was intended to make the statement that we were investing in our youth and the future of Jacksonville.

⚖

"Wow! Sheriff Glover, I don't ever want to be on the ballot against you!" I will never forget those fourteen words, for they were spoken before hundreds of my fellow Jacksonville citizens by President Bill Clinton. It was September 19, 1995, and President Clinton and I had just walked the length of Marvin Avenue in inner-city Jacksonville. This was one of the 408 neighborhood walks I took as sheriff, 51 per year during each of my eight years in office. Many were noteworthy, but none more than this one.

Joined by then governor Lawton Chiles, US Attorney General Janet Reno, and others, President Clinton and I discussed crime, policing, and a whole lot of other issues as we walked and interacted with area residents. The Northside neighborhood of Carvill Park had received federal funding for a community policing program, and we were there to measure its implementation, results, and popularity.

After that walk, I had the honor of standing before the crowd in Carvill Park and introducing President Clinton. This is part of what I said:

> When I was elected sheriff, I pledged to you that I was going to increase police presence on the street, reduce the level of fear in this community, and get you involved in law enforcement, and I want to tell you that this 1994 crime bill has assisted me in achieving those

goals. One of my main focuses was to increase the number of police officers on the street as a preventative measure to stifle crime.

The program is working well in Carvill Park, and we will spread that same spirit throughout this city. I also pledged that I would not just sit behind my desk and read reports and surveys on crime—I would go to the neighborhoods, and every neighborhood would be my office. And I've kept that pledge.

You know, people said that Jacksonville would never get an NFL team, and people said that Nat Glover would never be elected Jacksonville sheriff. The message we want to send to the country today, in the presence of our president, is that in Jacksonville, we can do anything.

In return, President Clinton spoke about crime and the crime bill that was starting to work. He said, "What I want you to know is that, just like Sheriff Glover said that Jacksonville could do anything, America can do this. We do not have to put up with the high rates of crime we have. We do not have to put up with the high rates of drug abuse among our children we have. We can do something about it. You have evidence on this street, in this neighborhood. We can do something about it."

I couldn't agree more, and we did do something. We brought crime rates down, and community policing was a big part of that. The Secret Service, by the way, had asked me to disarm my officers who were on stage that day with President Clinton. I refused, politely but firmly. For one thing, we shared responsibility with the president's bodyguards. And, importantly, I could not and would not insult my officers like that.

My neighborhood walks often included an entourage of my officers, who were joined by community leaders and members of the media. We walked quickly, covering as much ground as possible while also carefully observing and listening. The process soon earned the nickname "fast-walk-chatter." I cannot deny that the publicity was certainly beneficial to my career, but far more importantly, it visibly demonstrated that I would go directly to the citizens rather than going to my staff for updates on local situations and for details of any issues that had arisen.

In a nutshell, we showed that the sheriff's department, from the top down, cared. I just wanted to send a message that "You can count on me." I wanted to demonstrate that I cared about the community before an inevitable crisis requiring community support occurred.

During the early phases of my tenure, we also created Sheriff's Advisory Councils (ShAdCos) in every sector of the city. Another element of my push toward community policing was that these councils consisted of local citizens concerned about their neighborhoods. The JSO organized and maintained the councils so we could ensure continual input from citizens. The JSO's zone commander for each region chaired these meetings.

As I moved through my first term as sheriff, the ShAdCos continued to grow, as did the input they provided about what was going on in their communities. Each patrol division held an annual meeting of all the ShAdCos to share information about crime rates and strategies used to suppress crime. At the end of each year, the patrol divisions would host a joint ShAdCos meeting attended by approximately four hundred to five hundred members. At this meeting, I would present my "State of the ShAdCos" message and answer questions from members. The meeting would conclude with me presenting a gavel to the incoming chairperson of each ShAdCos.

At the outset of this project, many of my JSO officers expressed doubt over the citizens' ongoing commitment to these councils, but I told them that if these citizens did not meet us halfway, we would make up the difference through our own decisions and actions. My confidence was soon rewarded. Most citizen members devoted considerable energy and input, and the councils remain to this day a pivotal component of JSO's policing strategy.

In addition, we created the Crisis Intervention Training (CIT) program to help officers deal with emotionally disturbed people. Increasingly aware of the need, I became even more determined to create this program in the wake of a fatal police shooting of a mentally ill woman. We worked with mental health providers and required all our officers to get mental health training to handle people with mental health problems.

We fortified the department's commitment to the Police Athletic League (PAL), traditionally an effective way of uniting neighborhood youth and police officers for a common purpose. We constructed a new building for the PAL, setting the group apart from other youth-serving organizations in our community, and it still engages hundreds of kids every year. These relationships became transformational for participating officers and kids, giving everyone involved the opportunity to grow stronger together.

Civil service rules were put in place to protect government workers. They are designed to keep order, prevent favoritism, and also to prevent unqualified individuals from getting jobs they are not prepared for. Therefore, civil service exams were put in place to test the knowledge of all individuals interested in moving up in rank. The promotion list is a simple list of the names ranked by test score, from highest to lowest. From a resource management perspective, my administration implemented a process called "The Rule of Three," intended to provide some latitude on promotions. It allowed the sheriff to select from the top three candidates on the civil service promotion list. This allowed me to not just robotically promote the person with the highest score on a battery of tests, though aptitude was certainly important.

Additionally, I wanted to elevate the most suitable candidate based on diversity in demographics, skills, knowledge, and other experience. Our process also allowed me to consider past disciplinary issues and, importantly, to seed management with previously underrepresented minority and female officers.

I had a police officer who was not exactly one of my fans. He had the audacity to attach to his personal car a drawing of a little boy (also known as Calvin peeing) urinating on the words "Nat Glover." He was disciplined by his superiors and ordered to remove the decal. Now, flash forward a few years. The guy was up for promotion, and he appeared in my office to apologize for his past behavior. While I initially considered passing him over, I decided to do some background checking on him to assess his character and identify any possible patterns of behavior. I wanted to evaluate whether he would be the type of officer who was so audacious as to disrespect his subordinates that he would be a menace to civilians, particularly Black civilians. I was rather pleased not to find any pattern of behavior that would have led me to that conclusion. So I assured him that I would not hold his ugly past against him and eventually promoted him. My actions were consistent with my belief never to initiate reprisals against people who had offended me, particularly if they showed true remorse.

In another action, I made it clear that I was relying on my undersheriff and had deputized him to serve in my name and with my authority as required. I had built my cabinet by creating a team of rivals with diverse perspectives. My first undersheriff, John Gordon, had initially supported one of my white opponents during the election. But no matter—he was one of the smartest people I had ever met, possessing an uncanny ability to solve the most difficult problems with a direct, no-nonsense approach. We made a great team. He understood that to be successful, I needed to win the confidence and favor of an overwhelmingly white police force, and Undersheriff Gordon, who is white, created opportunities for me to do just that. For example, if he felt it necessary to fire an officer, he sometimes quietly let me know that an action by me to reverse that termination and instead impose a thirty-day suspension would not be resented by him and would, in fact, help me build support within the ranks. He never pouted or complained, even when I took actions with which he didn't agree. Undersheriff Gordon was a great all-around person, a key factor in any success I might have achieved as sheriff, and I always will be grateful to him.

I managed to get dozens of officers out from behind their desks and back on the street—and to hire additional officers. A number of these people thought they had earned these no-risk desk jobs. I said, "No, I need you on the streets. This desk work amounts to clerical duties, and we can hire clerks to do them." Within a year of my election, 199 more officers were reporting to the patrol division's roll call every morning. As part of my strategy to increase police presence in our communities, I ordered new restrictions on the number of officers who could eat in the same restaurant at the same time. That action was meant to diminish the opportunities for the bad guys to recognize the pattern that at a certain time of day, most of the officers in the area would be eating at the same restaurant, which would reduce the coverage and police presence at that time. That was not an initially popular move on my part, but the workforce eventually saw the wisdom in it and accepted it.

Before my first term in office, we suffered through an apparent epidemic of questionable actions by our officers. As director of police services, my responsibilities included human resources, which meant hiring, firing, and everything in between. This was a difficult time for all of us, and a grand jury ultimately recommended significant improvements in recruitment, hiring, training, and discipline. The sheriff at that time, Jim McMillan, asked me to come back with recommendations from a committee I had put together on how to address these issues. We all worked on the situation, and the improvement program was handed over to me when I became sheriff. One of our recommendations was to raise the educational requirement for new officers from holding a high school diploma to having a college degree (with later exceptions for military veterans and officers who had served in other departments).

This enhanced educational policy met with considerable resistance within JSO, but I pushed it through, and I'm very proud of that achievement. Despite tremendous pressure, I was not going to back off from the educational requirement. It was the right thing to do. Hiring officers with a college degree meant they likely were exposed to the social sciences and humanities courses—as well as to other students—that would give them an edge in dealing with diverse populations.

Despite the many protests, I was confident that anyone who really wanted to become a police officer would find a way. Police officers must be exceptional because they can take a life when they make a unilateral decision based on a momentary situational assessment. We simply must seek and hire the highest caliber of police officers. The enormity of their responsibilities demands nothing less.

I continued to get other pushback on certain decisions, particularly my order that officers limit their hours of secondary employment—most often security positions at commercial sites, sports events, and so forth. The objective here was to make certain they were properly rested while on the job as officers, so I ordered a 90 hours per month limit on outside work and increased it to 120 hours per month during the holiday season. Many officers believed, not unreasonably, that I had made plenty of money this way as a uniformed officer, so why couldn't they? Why was I taking money out of their pockets? But, again, the safety of my officers was at the forefront of my thinking. Having worked too long at their secondary jobs, too often they were tired and agitated when they reported to work for all the citizens of Jacksonville. Among other things, I became concerned about their alertness, a lack of which could jeopardize their safety and the safety of others.

I also received a number of letters from citizens whose vehicles had broken down on our streets, highways, and expressways. These people reported that JSO patrol cars would just pass by, not stopping to offer aid or not even just slowing down to assess the situation. We were allowing officers to take their JSO vehicles home to provide a presence in their neighborhoods and, obviously, help stranded citizens, even when the officers were off duty. As was common for me, I felt that a mere reiteration of our policy would be insufficient without actual evidence of implementation. So I ordered the inspections unit to collect data. For example, the unit would leave a confiscated car on the side of a frequently traveled road a confiscated car with its hood up to indicate distress. Inspection unit officers documented a number of patrol vehicles that did not stop. We called in those officers and had ... discussions about this. Some had their take-home vehicle privileges suspended. The lesson was learned—and not just by those officers.

The result of this attempt to hold our police accountable was that I soon began receiving appreciative letters from the public complimenting our officers—often in more than one patrol car—for stopping to ensure that the motorists were all right.

Shifting to another topic, I did not hesitate to promote an openly gay female officer, Carol Hladki, to assistant chief. Unfortunately, this was not a popular move at the time. The LGBTQ community was forced to hide in the closet to remain safe in a hostile environment. Carol was concerned about me and my reputation if I promoted her. I was concerned about living with myself if I did not promote her. I was so impressed by her selflessness, bravery, and courage in sharing with me that she was gay and considering any potential pushback I would receive in elevating her. And if she could be fearless, so could I. The lesson learned for me was to always try to put people in positions that allow them to prove themselves and will give them a space where they will shine. Carol retired as director of police services, the third-highest rank in the JSO's entire hierarchy.

Here's what Carol says about the opportunities that were opened to her:

It's obviously a patriarchy-type profession, and it certainly was then—maybe 95 percent white male, 5 percent female. Women were looked at differently, and we worried about it. Were we tokens? Were we taking a man's position? The fact that Nat wanted a diverse team, and not only of gender and race, that he wanted to bring together a team that looked like the community was really something. I hadn't even supported Nat for sheriff, and he reached out to promote me and make females so much more visible in the department. I just think the world of Nat Glover.

And I think the world of Carol Hladki.

Finally, this brings me to one of our most important accomplishments. Before my election, then-sheriff Jim McMillan often met with department captains, who enjoyed the benefits of being in civil service positions, which had significant protection against termination through the backing of unions. The sheriff would give these captains direct orders to address crime in a certain manner. While in the room with the sheriff, these individuals would passively nod in agreement, but when they left the meeting, things were quite different.

On more than one occasion, they would meet in the third-floor snack bar, which became known as "The Captains' Round Table," to discuss the "nonsense" the sheriff directed them to accomplish. Oftentimes, this resulted in their direct defiance of the sheriff's leadership and direction, acts that came perilously close to mutiny. These captains would literally say, "I am civil service–protected. What is he going to do—fire me?" And they were *right*!

Jacksonville had a strong civil service system, and it was extremely difficult to terminate an employee, even if they were directly defying the wishes of the sheriff. This was a problem I recognized early in my campaign and an issue I was determined to correct. As a result, one of my many campaign promises was to create a newly appointed rank of assistant chief that would basically eliminate the need for the civil service rank of captain. Once elected, I went through the legislative process to create this new position. I did not demote or terminate any of the career civil service captains. They were reassigned, and, in some cases, I did promote a few of the worthiest ones to my initial staff as assistant chiefs. Through attrition, the rank of captain eventually faded away.

The necessity for this move was evident, and I was not afraid to make it. The sheriff is elected to serve and protect the community in the manner he or she thinks is best. For any of my community initiatives to be implemented, individuals needed to remain disciplined and loyal to the direction of their commanders. The new rank had to be created to ensure that the very best police services were being performed by the men and women of the agency. This is exactly what our community deserved.

My leadership philosophy dictated that I should treat everyone in JSO leadership positions and throughout the ranks equally. Treating everyone in the same way provides a fair opportunity for them to succeed and strive for distinction. I also had no problem rewarding performance with merit pay increases. It's a two-way street, and we are required to reward excellent performance. When I decided to award or not award merit pay to a particular officer or leader, I was ready for their questions: "Why me?" or "Why not me?" My sincere response would be, "I'm glad you asked," and then I would tell them why they deserved a raise or not. I considered this a fair question and worthy of a considered response. I wanted to be sure I was approachable and that all my subordinates felt empowered to ask questions and express themselves. The open dialogue also opened the door to discussing ways to improve performance.

To be honest, during my early years as sheriff, I was under enormous pressure. When you're the *only* anything, you're under constant scrutiny. Much of my unease, however, was largely self-imposed. I felt, with justification, that I would not be allowed a single significant misstep. A certain portion of the community, however tiny, was eager to see me fail, so I refused to entertain even the possibility of failure. I recognized that such failure would have significant ramifications that might persist for decades, and not just for me. Now, don't get me wrong—this came at a cost. My commitment and ambition did deprive me of time with my family. But I give thanks to God for covering for me because they were always supportive and understanding. If I had to advise someone with such ambition today, I would tell them to find a way to distinguish themselves from their peers. Give people a reason to speak highly of you, recognize your distinction, and honor your legacy. Nothing worth having is going to be easy, and it will always come at a cost. I believed then and still believe today that going after your dream is worth the cost, and I don't have any pause on that.

Like it or not, I was now representing not just my Black community and not just as the first elected Black sheriff in the Deep South since the Reconstruction Era. I also now symbolized the hopes and dreams of countless Black officers and young people. I could not let them down. Failure was not an option; mediocrity also was not an option. Consequently, I had to perform to the highest of my personal and professional standards, and I had no choice but to keep an eye on my public image. Among many other things, I had to tactfully sidestep obvious flirtations from women notwithstanding race, which I would have done anyway, given my marriage vows. I knew that I had to wake up every morning and please pretty much everyone—the public, police officers, politicians, and reporters.

Back then, paper carriers still would deliver newspapers every morning. Newspaper circulation was still strong and, in many neighborhoods, the main news source.

Beginning the day after I was elected, I awakened every morning and stepped outside to pick up the paper that had been tossed on my driveway or lawn. I needed to know what was being said about my administration and about me. I recognized that positive news stories were good for my administration and would provide greater opportunities for us to complete our ambitious agenda. Thus, these stories became my barometer and sometimes my crutch. A positive news story would validate; a negative news story would alarm.

One morning, as I anxiously grabbed the paper, which was my yardstick for validation, I recognized the deficiency in my thinking. I had spent a lifetime trusting my gut, abilities, and my God-given talents. Why would I cede that to the vagaries of news coverage? So I stopped reading the newspaper and being governed by its content. I started to rely on my own instincts and my experience. And it worked. My zeal and energy grew. My outlook improved, and my performance exceeded expectations by any measure. I was determined not to let the voices and opinions of strangers shape my definition of success or failure. I would do the job that only I could do.

There were, however, other methods I relied upon to gauge the public's view of my administration. It was clear that pollsters had been running more frequent job satisfaction surveys during my tenure as sheriff. Nevertheless, my approval ratings were always in the eighties and sometimes the nineties. I couldn't ask for more than that. But I did. The JCCI (Jacksonville Community Council Incorporated) conducted an annual quality of life survey. One of the questions on that survey was, "Do you feel safe walking in your neighborhood at night?" I would monitor those statistics for each section of the city. If they were lower in a certain sector, I would bring it to the attention of the specific command officer in that area during staff meetings that included their peers. I needed to demonstrate that I was watching the surveys carefully, which in turn compelled the command officers to do the same. The goal was ultimately to use this as a motivating factor, and it worked.

We had our setbacks, too, of course.

My son, Officer Michael Glover, and two other officers were accused of beating a confession out of a fifteen-year-old suspect after he allegedly killed a tourist. I never hesitate to talk about the incident, as painful as it might be, and I was the one who called for an investigation of the interrogation and arrest of the juvenile. The officers were thoroughly questioned, underwent expert polygraph testing, and had their backgrounds combed through. After all of this, there were no findings of any wrongdoing. Additionally, the grand jury came to the same conclusion. But I also know my son well. He had no history of violence—either on the force or otherwise. In fact, he has a rather calm demeanor. But he was the son of the sheriff, and it became a big news story.

Amid the media explosion, Michael came to me and said he felt it was in everyone's best interest if he resigned. He also felt that his presence was affecting not just him and me but also the officers with whom he worked. I did not want him to resign, but it was his choice. He was an excellent homicide detective—diligent and always cleared his cases. I left it up to him whether to resign, and he did. He now works as a private investigator. The young man who had been arrested was acquitted, and the city paid his family $775,000 to settle a lawsuit.

As sheriff, I wanted to make a difference. I wanted to make certain that the public knew I had their backs. With more officers on the street and with successful applications for three federal community policing grants, arrests increased by double digits while crimes diminished by 8 percent during my first six months in office and by quite a bit more as time passed. We bought new mobile community policing vehicles, a new computer-aided dispatching system (the first in seventeen years), upgraded mobile data terminal systems (putting statewide criminal justice information at officers' fingertips), and an upgraded automated fingerprint identification system. We also created a toll-free line for victims to receive updates on inmates. All of this, and more, brought us quite a bit of recognition.

Personally, I was honored to receive the Great Floridian Award in 2016 for my dedication to the city of Jacksonville through law enforcement (and education). I only grasped the significance of this when I reviewed the list of other awardees, among them former governor and US senator Bob Graham and Walt Disney. I also was inducted in 2021 into the state's Law Enforcement Officers Hall of Fame, a true honor. But I'm probably most proud of this recognition for my department. When I served as sheriff, the department received the Distinguishable Law Enforcement Triple Crown Accreditation Award. The National Sheriffs' Association established this rare honor to recognize departments that achieve simultaneous accreditation by the Commission on the Accreditation of Law Enforcement Agencies, the American Correctional Association's Commission on Accreditation for Corrections, and the National Commission on Correctional Health Care. Achieving this is a daunting task. Since the establishment of the award in 1993, fewer than one hundred sheriff's offices have qualified—out of more than three thousand departments. I was honored to be the leader of a team that earned this national honor, and I remain humbled by my team's accomplishments.

Those achievements occurred because I firmly believe that in law enforcement, you cannot be successful without community support. It has been my experience that community involvement is a valuable investment that will pay great dividends if you can convince the community you are sincere and not just checking the boxes. The return on that investment will have redeeming value if you have a crisis because the community will be prepared to answer your call for assistance if you so request. In addition to the citizen advisory councils and the community and neighborhood walks we implemented, here are a few more notable community initiatives we began in Jacksonville, which other cities might want to consider:

- **Citizen Academy:** Citizens signed up for a ten-week course, one night a week, that provided them with insight into the work done by the sheriff's office.

- **Stop Stations:** These venues were usually an office space in a business or a room in a residence provided by the owner. They provided beat officers with privacy and the ability to access those conveniences while facilitating his/her report-writing and other general duties. Some conveniences included restrooms, telephones, writing desks, and office supplies. The availability of options varied among stop stations.

- **Victim Information Notification Everyday (VINE) System:** This system automatically notified victims of crimes such as stalking, domestic violence, and sexual battery, along with families of murder victims, of when the perpetrator was released or transferred from the Department of Corrections. This notification enabled victims to maintain a sense of security. It also facilitated communication with the sheriff's office on a continuing basis concerning the status of the criminals responsible for their crimes.

- **Summer Youth Intervention Program:** This summer program targeted youth between the ages of twelve and seventeen who were considered at risk for becoming involved in criminal activity or who had been mandated by the judicial system. In this program, the youth were led by police officers through structured activities in the classroom, on the athletic field, or at military or civilian educational sites. Activities were designed to develop positive attitudes and life skills. Emphasis was placed upon social skills, respect for others, self-esteem, conflict resolution, self-discipline, team building, and leadership.

- **Neighborhood Cleanups:** I personally participated in every neighborhood cleanup that occurred during my administration. These cleanups were organized and carried out to improve the appearance of neighborhoods littered with debris and trash and instilling more pride in the community. During the cleanups, I'd often find myself working alongside incarcerated individuals. I wanted to show these individuals that I saw them as more than inmates and recognized their humanity, and in speaking with them, I learned as much from them as they learned from me. We also had city agencies and department personnel address certain regulatory problems we might encounter during a cleanup, such as animal control, zoning, trash pickup, and other issues for which city department personnel were required.
- **Weekly TV Program:** To add to the perception of full disclosure, I initiated a weekly cable television program titled *Signal 94*. The program was hosted by the sheriff's office public information coordinator. Viewers had the opportunity to monitor everything going on in the sheriff's office. We had guest speakers, professional experts, and call-in capability from the viewers. I wanted members of my cabinet to be prepared to present the sheriff office's perspective in any area for which they were responsible.

But my proudest achievement since my breakthrough election and reelection (I received 81 percent of the vote for my second term) is the fact that during my administration, there was a 17 percent reduction in crime in Jacksonville over eight years. Since then, Black sheriffs have been elected in the Florida counties of Alachua, Orange, Gadsden, Leon, and Clay. In addition, a Black sheriff was appointed to serve out the term of a disgraced sheriff in populous Broward County (Fort Lauderdale). He was later elected to the office. And in Jacksonville, more than 30 percent of the current sheriff's command staff is African American.

But I am also proud that of the top five people on my command staff, four out of the five possessed a master's degree, evidencing what I said before: I have seen the difference that education makes for individuals and organizations. I can think of no better legacy of striving for justice and am grateful for it.

CHAPTER 12

CRIMINAL JUSTICE AND INJUSTICE

We found [a pause] Maddie Clifton this morning at about 7:30 a.m. [Another pause.] She was dead.

I t's inevitable in my line of work: police officers sometimes see the best of human behavior and character, but we spend most of our time dealing with the worst of human behavior and character. Sometimes, "the worst" plumbs so low that it defeats our ability to describe it. Still, we must deal with it—and, as sheriff, I too often found myself having to share descriptions of terrible crimes with the public.

Facing the challenge of full disclosure versus the human need to protect the privacy of victims and the needs of relatives, friends, and survivors dealing with unimaginable horror was an element of the job I simply hated.

One particular case just broke my heart. At 5:00 p.m. on November 3, 1998, Sheila Clifton reported her daughter missing from their Lakewood neighborhood on Jacksonville's Southside. The girl, Madlyn Rae Clifton, was only eight years old. A bright-eyed, freckle-faced girl with an easy smile, Maddie loved basketball and playing for the local YMCA team, and she wore the number 5 on her team jersey.

We responded quickly, blocking all exits and entrances from her neighborhood. We checked every vehicle leaving and entering. We conducted house-to-house searches. National Guard troops and more than four hundred volunteers, some from distant areas, responded as the days passed, combing the area. We came up dry. No sign of Maddie, and no communication from a would-be kidnapper. Nothing. The disappearance and the search became national—even international—news.

During the shutdown of the neighborhood, I was confronted with a dilemma. One of my chiefs wanted to reopen the neighborhood to normal traffic flow. The other chief wanted to continue the shutdown, checking cars traveling in and out of the neighborhood. He was convinced Madlyn was still in one of those houses. I settled the dispute by deciding to keep the neighborhood shut down. As it later turned out, we were right. Her body was still in one of those houses.

After a week of searching, we discovered the unimaginable. Melissa Phillips, the mother of Joshua Phillips, who lived across the street from Maddie and was one of her playmates, smelled an odor and saw what she thought was a leak under her son's waterbed. There, wedged into the base of Joshua's bed, placed in a fetal position and bound with tape, were the battered remains of young Maddie. To her credit, Mrs. Phillips called us. We rushed over. The body had always been there, but our searchers had missed it, given its unusual location.

The word "gruesome" doesn't begin to describe what we found. Maddie had been beaten with a baseball bat, strangled, and stabbed. Fourteen-year-old Joshua told us that he had accidentally hit her in the head with a ball as they played. When she wouldn't stop crying, fearing a violent reaction from his own father, he beat her into silence—and death. I had no choice but to conduct a press conference to share this news. But how do you do this with sensitivity and empathy? I nearly burst into tears when I announced: "We found [a pause] Maddie Clifton this morning at about 7:30 a.m. [Another pause.] She was dead."

Maddie's parents were, of course, devastated. So were the rest of us—the officers who had been working the case and the vast number of people who had been following it. Hearing my words live, neighbors and others who had been searching for the girl sobbed, screamed, and fell to their knees in sorrow and despair.

This is how Jennifer Waugh, a veteran Jacksonville TV news reporter and anchor, recalls that awful scene:

> I remember that day as if it were yesterday. Watching the sheriff walk down the middle of the street from the command center, you could hear a pin drop. When the sheriff made the announcement, "We found Maddie Clifton ... she was dead," the crowd gasped in horror. The woman—a bystander—standing next to me started weeping and collapsed into someone. I'll never forget that look on her face.

Joshua Phillips was ultimately convicted of first-degree murder and sentenced to life in prison without the possibility of parole. It was a harsh sentence for such a young man and attracted some criticism. I'm still not sure how I feel about it, though I know this: the case came as close as any to breaking me. As I said some years ago, "I always felt like if I could make the children and the senior citizens safe, everyone in between would be OK." But I also know this: the lives of two young people were destroyed on November 3, 1998.

Pop Warner is the world's largest and oldest youth football, cheer, and dance program, typically serving 325,000 kids ages five to sixteen years old every year. It is one of the few such organizations that require participants to meet high academic standards to stay in the program. Thus, it attracts some of our best kids and most devoted parents.

One afternoon in the predominantly Black Northwest section of Jacksonville, Johnnie Gatlin, age fifty-four, picked up her two nephews, Deon Kirkland, age thirteen, and his twelve-year-old brother, Chris, from Pop Warner football practice. They arrived home, Johnnie parked the car, and all seemed well. It was just another evening for the family. But the moment she parked the car, another car came screeching along-side her. Two men wielding automatic weapons fired numerous bullets at Gatlin's parked car, gunning the family down. It was a revenge killing—but it targeted the wrong people. In a terrible case of mistaken identity, Johnnie and her two nephews were killed instantly.

Johnnie's body was slumped over the steering wheel when we arrived at the scene. The boys were strewn in the back seat, still wearing their uniforms. Bullets had broken and almost amputated the little boys' arms. One of the boys had been playing a video game in the back seat, and he still had the console in his hand when we found his body. Even for me, a seasoned police officer, it was a horribly grotesque scene. I was at the point of despair, my eyes burning as I pushed back tears. My internal emotions were spiraling out of control as I attempted to rationalize this horrific tableau. Had I, the sheriff, somehow let down these little boys? If someone else had been sheriff, would this have happened?

TV reporter Jennifer Waugh said, "Maddie's death and the shooting death of two young boys killed in the back seat of their car . . . are the only two times in all my years working with Nat that I saw him visibly shaken."

Based on our early investigation, it seemed clear that the gunmen were drug dealers who had been targeting the boys' uncle. The now-deceased family had been driving the uncle's car.

A press conference conducted by a sheriff or other law enforcement official requires an artful combination of communicating accurate facts that inform the public along with messages to the suspects still at large. So during that first all-important meeting with the media, I looked—more to the point, I glared—into the camera and said to the suspects, "I know you are running." I then raised my voice. "But more importantly, I know you will be arrested. I know you are running, but rest assured, we are coming."

Later, I conducted a follow-up press conference to share the suspects' names and urge them to surrender. One almost immediately turned himself in to the JSO, and we arrested the second suspect soon after. Incidentally, that was a tactic I used when I knew the suspect's identity. I would urge the parents of the suspect to make sure that they come in and surrender because I did not want other officers who might not be as sympathetic to hurt or possibly kill a resisting suspect. I have gotten tips from parents who did not want to see their sons or grandsons hurt. So when the suspect walked into the Police Memorial Building, he said that Sheriff Glover had told him to come in. I learned later that his mother or grandmother had heard the news conference and urged him to come in and surrender.

The case, as horrendous as it was, as haunting as it remains, gave me an opportunity to demonstrate my clear intention to pursue criminals, a critical quality to any success as a sheriff.

⚖️

In another case, on July 10, 1998, a woman pretending to be a nurse dawdled in the maternity ward of what now is called UF Health Jacksonville. That woman, Gloria Williams, kidnapped eight-hours-old Kamiyah Mobley from her bassinet—boldly snatching her from her parents—walked out of the hospital, and disappeared with the child.

We searched the hospital and surrounding area. We dispatched helicopters for an aerial view. We established roadblocks. Nothing. The woman and the kidnapped baby had vanished.

Over the next eighteen years, thousands of investigative leads poured in, but none proved helpful. Finally, two productive leads arrived in late 2016, and in January 2017, Kamiyah was found alive in Walterboro, South Carolina. She was now eighteen years old and pretty darned surprised to find out she was not who she thought she was. DNA testing proved that she was not Alexis K. Manigo, daughter of Gloria (Williams) Manigo of Walterboro, South Carolina. She was actually Kamiyah Mobley, daughter of Shanara Mobley and Craig Aiken of Jacksonville, Florida.

Although we were not able to find Kamiyah during my term as sheriff, I am proud that the continuity of leadership at the JSO and across state lines allowed JSO sheriff Mike Williams to locate her. By the way, Gloria (Williams) Manigo was sentenced to eighteen years in prison for kidnapping young Kamiyah. And as a result of the abduction, hospitals in Jacksonville and beyond significantly enhanced security in their maternity wards.

⚖️

At one point, an unruly inmate was killed in our jail, choked to death by a guard who applied a neck restraint by wrapping his arm around the inmate's throat. Several other officers also were involved in the incident. With so many officers on the scene and dealing with the prisoner, why had such drastic and ultimately deadly action been taken? I reprimanded the officers involved, particularly the one in charge and the one who applied the neck restraint. I really wanted to fire that guy. He was an officer who had been assigned to another floor and was called because he had a reputation for getting compliance from inmates. I was so disappointed because I knew something was wrong. If I had multiple officers on the scene trying to control one inmate and the inmate ended up dead, that raised a significant red flag in my mind. But the officer went to arbitration, the process that I described earlier as often counterproductive to effective discipline of officers. He won his case and was sent back to work.

I was disappointed, to say the least. I still believed that the application of the restraining hold (lateral vascular neck restraint) was excessive, but I told his commanding officers not to be harsh with him. For the rest of his life, he would have to carry the guilt of having killed someone. No need for us to hold any further grudges. In the end, that fellow became a model officer, though the incident remained etched into my brain for years to come. I felt there should be ways to restrain someone other than the lateral vascular neck restraint—commonly known as a choke hold—that, without precise expert application, can kill someone within seconds. I looked for the right moment and ultimately banned this inhumane hold. It was—and it remains—one step in the long journey toward improving police procedures and reforming the criminal justice system.

I never employed the choke hold, and I always found a way to do my job without drawing my weapon with the intent to shoot someone.

CHAPTER 13

CRIMINAL JUSTICE REFORM: CHANGE IS COMING AND OVERDUE

A right way and a wrong way. Killing civilians is the wrong way.

In 2016, an emotionally impaired and naked seventeen-year-old youth named David Joseph ran toward Officer Geoffrey Freeman of the Austin, Texas, police department. Saying that he feared for his life, Freeman shot the youth dead. Art Acevedo, then Austin's chief of police, met with community leaders and held a joint news conference with them. Then he fired Officer Freeman, accusing him of employing excessive force. The police union objected, as did many of Acevedo's command officers.

In a secretly recorded meeting with his command staff, Acevedo told them this:

The union got all pissed off because I fired Freeman. Some of you might have gotten pissed off. I'm going to tell you right now if we have another Freeman tomorrow, that is what's going to happen.

I didn't lose a minute of sleep. If you can't handle a kid in broad daylight, naked, and your first instinct is to come out with your gun, and your next instinct is to shoot the kid dead, you don't need to be a cop. I don't give a shit how nice you are.

We have got to raise our game. You are commanders. If you don't like it, you can move on, or you can demote. I'm not going to hold that against anybody if it's not for you, but we have got to step up.

I might have used somewhat different language in that situation, but I certainly agree with the sentiment. For police officers, there is a right way and a wrong way. Killing civilians is the wrong way. According to a credible study by a criminal justice expert, about one thousand Americans are killed by police officers every year. We simply must step up to do the right thing.

Art Acevedo went on to command the much larger Houston police force, developing a national reputation for, among other things, terminating rogue officers, saying exactly what was on his mind, and embracing social justice and the communities being policed by his officers. Then in early 2021, he took over—for what turned out to be just a brief period of time—the Miami Police Department, a force that experienced so many thorny problems with the surrounding community that it had just come out from under federal vigilance. And he got right down to business.

"We will not tolerate mediocrity at the Miami Police Department," Acevedo said during his very first news conference. "And I will not apologize for getting rid of mediocrity because when you allow mediocrity to fester, the community sees it. They know it, and it spreads like cancer."

I have already expressed my concerns over hiring and discipline practices at many—probably most—police departments in this nation. Still, I want to emphasize that reforming the US criminal justice system obviously must start at its initial point of contact with our citizens: policing. To this day, too many departments cling to a bar too low when it comes to hiring. Cedric L. Alexander, a member of President Obama's Task Force on 21st Century Policing, agreed with me. Alexander, who also served as director of public safety for DeKalb County, Georgia, part of the Atlanta metropolitan area, captured a key point in a March 2021 essay for the *Washington Post*. He noted that most police departments use standard and important criteria in hiring, including such things as a clean criminal record, test performance, and physical fitness, but that these leave out a critical factor:

> *Call it, if you will, heart.*
>
> *By heart, I mean a deep empathy that prompts you to act—in the moment and righteously. In some four decades of work in law enforcement, I have seen heart work the miracles of service and valor police officers perform daily. I have also seen deficiency, corruption, or absence of heart create the kind of tragedy and failure that killed [George] Floyd and that marked much of what occurred at Capitol Hill [during the insurrection] on Jan. 6.*

Tragedy and failure and lack of heart. It never seems to end. Some officers never seem to learn. In the wake of the George Floyd killing in Minneapolis, hundreds of police departments throughout the country found themselves confronting major protests. Too many of these police forces failed—and failed miserably.

The *New York Times* studied more than a dozen after-action reports conducted by departments in American cities, big and small. The findings were appalling. "In city after city," the *Times* reported:

. . . the reports are a damning indictment of police forces that were poorly trained, heavily militarized, and stunningly unprepared for the possibility that large numbers of people would surge into the streets, moved by the graphic images of Mr. Floyd's death under a police officer's knee.

The mistakes transcended geography, staffing levels, and financial resources. From midsize departments like the one in Indianapolis to big-city forces like New York City's, from top commanders to officers on the beat, police officers nationwide were unprepared to calm the summer's unrest. Their approaches consistently did the opposite. In many ways, the problems highlighted in the reports are fundamental to modern American policing, a demonstration of the aggressive tactics that had infuriated many of the protesters, to begin with.

And nothing was learned in the immediate aftermath. Nine months after a police officer suffocated George Floyd in Minneapolis, some officers in Los Angeles exchanged Valentine's Day cards with Floyd's photo and these words: "You take my breath away."

Policing in America is in crisis. Too many officers are too cynical and, at the same time, too enamored of the increasingly heavy weaponry available to them. To be fair, they also increasingly and understandably fear for their lives. So many guns are on our streets, carried by so many people with deadened souls and warped values. During an interview with the *New York Times*, US senator Bernie Sanders, D-Vermont, who also is a former mayor, placed the countervailing tensions in clear focus:

A cop's life is a difficult life. Schedules are terrible. Salaries, in many cases, are inadequate. It's a dangerous job. It's a job with a lot of pressure. We need to significantly improve training for the police. In certain communities, what is going on is absolutely unacceptable. It

must be changed, period. We cannot have racism in policing. If you
go to Black or Latino communities, they want this protection.

Well said. But I have more experience with the criminal justice system than most people, and I am here to tell you that needed reforms extend far beyond that initial point of contact between police and suspects.

When it comes to our zeal to incarcerate, and many other elements of the criminal justice system, the disparities between the United States and other nations are stark—and depressing. With statistics trending toward two million people behind bars, the US has the highest number of prisoners in the world, sometimes trading places with China for the number-one spot. However, the US has the highest prison population rate in the world, with approximately 655 prisoners per every 100,000 people. This is simply absurd; it is unacceptable, and it gets worse. Adjudication of cases is a particular problem, especially when it involves African Americans and other minorities—and often juveniles.

Many of us remember the case of Lionel Tate, a fourteen-year-old Black youth in South Florida who was sentenced to life in prison without parole for killing a six-year-old girl. Lionel became the youngest American in modern history to be sentenced to life in prison without the possibility of parole. As horrible as his crime was, many people, including then governor Jeb Bush, found the sentence excessive. I did too. We must always be sensitive to the rights and feelings of crime victims and their loved ones, but a forty-year sentence or anything else short of a life sentence for that boy would have delivered the same strong statement. What good does it do us to forfeit the life of another juvenile? That said, Tate turned out not to be the best example of the point. An appeals court overturned his sentence, but he went on to a life of crime and probation violations, and he ended up back in prison.

As illustrated by the Tate case, the system does not have enough advocates for offenders—people who can help offenders stop their lives of crime, find other paths, and assimilate more easily into law-abiding societies. It does not have enough minorities in positions of influence where their experiences and cultural sensitivities can do the most good. The system is not fair-minded, too often imposing far harsher sentences on people of color than on white Americans who commit identical crimes.

Disparities have been apparent for a long time in the treatment of various categories of offenders by prosecutors and judges, both categories overwhelmingly populated by white males. Decades of statistical analysis show that Black and Brown defendants clearly have suffered the effects of implicit bias when it comes to being charged, prosecuted, judged, and punished, although the inequities have decreased to some extent. According to a study by the Council on Criminal Justice, the disparity in imprisonment fell from 8.3–1 to 5.1–1 between 2000 to 2016; the Black/white disparity for drug crimes fell from 15–1 to 5–1; and the Black/white disparity among female offenders fell from 6–1 to 2–1. But even those statistics show that we have a long way to go.

In that *Florida Times-Union* column that I wrote shortly after the May 2020 police killing of George Floyd in Minneapolis, I said:

> *Suppose the biases are, in fact, implicit, meaning that the bias is unconscious. In that case, the whole notion of the pursuit of justice in our criminal justice system will need new, creative, and innovative approaches to the prosecution and sentencing process. In the absence of such reform, the results will be clear: justice is for whites only and a mere myth for others.*

I wrote then—and I believe now—that investigations of deadly encounters with police should be conducted not by local prosecutors, as generally is the case, but rather by a higher authority—an entity at the state or even the federal level.

That, plus significant structural, racial, and attitude changes throughout the criminal justice system, constitute merely initial steps toward achieving a more just justice system in this nation. Among many other things, governors who appoint judges to serve out the terms of elected judges must consider the proper balance of racial and other communities. As I wrote in that same column:

> We have come to a time in our history in minority households where women are terrified when their African American men leave the home. Even a trip to the grocery store or a routine errand elicits fear. Wives, mothers, sisters, and daughters all wait with bated breath until their husbands, sons, fathers, and brothers return home. Their fear and concerns are focused on the possibility of a routine police stop or detainment that could turn into a tragic confrontation, leaving their loved one dead on the side of the road. That fear—for the safety of Black males—is serious and real. It appears greater today than at any time in recent history and permeates the Black community. It is similar in magnitude to the fear created by the more explicit and threatening racism of the past against mostly Black males. Understanding this is fundamental to moving forward.

Again, I am convinced that when the system is reformed, with community input, it's going to be better for everyone. I believe there is tremendous redeeming value in the resurrection of community trust in the system. That is one of the reasons I have always wanted to be open about sharing my story. In many ways, I did not see my potential as being any greater than that of many other young men I crossed paths with as a police officer. At times, the line between success and failure for these young men seemed very thin, with no room for error because the justice system (for them) is unforgiving. I deeply believe that my story can be their story. But they also need help from the system—a system that needs to be reformed and purged of its implicit and explicit racism.

CHAPTER 14

LICENSE TO KILL, LICENSE TO SERVE: POLICE MUST REASSESS, RESET

I sometimes ask myself, *How did we get here?*

The criminal justice system is structured to distribute justice fairly and equitably. However, the actual application of justice is far from the perfect idea of how the system is supposed to work. It's intended to be a system of checks and balances. The judge and jury check the prosecutors, and the prosecutors check the police officers. But before we can begin to tackle the fundamental aspects of the checks and balances that should keep the scales of justice fair, balanced, and blind, we need to address the fact that the irresponsible application of the system, coupled with the disproportionate representation of Black people throughout the system, continues to perpetuate an environment of injustice to this demographic. Black judges make up approximately 5.5 percent of judges in the United States, and Black men make up approximately 35 percent of people in prison. How can there be fairness and equity in a system skewed in its representation?

My status as both a product of the Black ghetto and a former leader of a major law enforcement agency in the nation's Deep South affords me first-hand insight into the discussion around the challenges and opportunities within law enforcement. Put simply, the tragic, ugly, infuriatingly casual police murder on May 25, 2020, of George Floyd of Minneapolis served, among other things, as a key milestone in the historic and ongoing epidemic of police brutality against African Americans and as the catalyst of a new deeper and wider stage of the Black Lives Matter protest campaign. More to my point at the moment: it illustrated anew that we, the sound minds and experts in the criminal justice system, must confront, mitigate, and—no matter how difficult—strive to end implicit bias in the nation's police departments.

We must reeducate our police officers. We must drain racism wherever it secrets itself in these officers, as a physician drains the pus from an infection. We must reform these departments, sometimes from top to bottom, more often through efforts focused on mid-level superiors and the officers they supervise. Law enforcement officers of all types and at all ranks are understood to have a license to kill—legal authority to deploy deadly force unilaterally and at a moment's notice. This alone makes them unique in American society. At the same time, however, the unofficial, unlicensed rule of the Thin Blue Line too often protects misbehaving and rogue officers from the oversight of their fellow officers, undermining the integrity of—and trust in—law enforcement. This must cease.

Again, I say this not only as a Black man but as a sheriff who oversaw more than 2,200 police and correctional officers, most of them excellent, responsible, and color-blind, and some who were none of that. In doing so, I recognize that I am breaking with some of my colleagues in the upper management ranks of these departments. So be it.

It's worth restating that, on July 19, 2020, about two months after the murder of George Floyd and as protests still raged in many corners of the nation, I wrote for the *Florida Times-Union*, the primary news outlet in the Jacksonville area, an appraisal of the inherent racism poisoning many police departments, its venomous effect on Black communities, and my suggestions to neutralize that toxin.

> *I sometimes ask myself,* How did we get here? *A segment of our community worries more about a police confrontation than [about] the dangerous criminal elements present in our communities. In the past, there was no justice, no mercy, and no peace in Black communities. Are we there again?*

I noted in my op-ed that many police officers take their duties of protecting and serving seriously. They do not hesitate to protect citizens and the community at large, in many instances at great personal risk. At the same time, many—probably most—departments harbor a number of officers who are less professional, less helpful, more aggressive, and more prone to bias, prejudice, and outright racism. These officers usually manifest a variety of personality faults that trigger the tragedies that so often and so needlessly shatter Black families and surrounding communities.

Nearly every week brings us another disturbing case of apparent police brutality or other misconduct perpetrated against people of color or against other marginalized groups. Often—far too often—these officers have well-documented histories of abuse in their official roles or personal lives. And yet there they are, still carrying their badge and their weapons into the communities they despise.

In recent years, this problem has become compounded by the growing magnitude of political extremism within the general public and, more ominously, within law enforcement agencies.

The *New York Times* reported that at least thirty law enforcement officers participated in the January 6, 2021, rally in Washington, DC, that preceded and triggered the insurrectionist rampage at the Capitol. Several later were arrested on federal charges.

In addition, white supremacist groups have established footholds within police departments in many corners of the country. In Philadelphia alone, seventy-two officers were disciplined for racist social media posts in 2019.

"There is zero room, not only in society but more so in professions of public trust and service, for people to have extremist views, regardless of ideology," Houston Police Chief Art Acevedo, president of the Major Cities Chiefs Association, told the *New York Times*. And yet, many agencies remain infected by this virus.

A pioneering 2020 study by *Yale Law Journal* identified one factor behind this volatile phenomenon: officers who are fired or compelled to resign due to misconduct, extremism, or other malignancies too often are rehired by other police agencies. In Florida alone, more than one thousand of these troubled men and women—called "wandering officers"—patrol the streets yearly. In addition, they tend to end up in "smaller agencies with fewer resources in communities with slightly higher proportions of residents of color," according to the study. Even worse, these "wandering officers" are far more likely to be fired from the next job. "They are also more likely to receive complaints at the state licensing board for 'moral character violations,' including complaints for violent or sexual misconduct and for integrity-related misdeeds," the study found.

The Yale study examined employment records of all ninety-eight thousand full-time law enforcement officers in almost five hundred police agencies in Florida over thirty years, but the researchers said they believed their findings pointed to similar issues throughout the nation. Other experts point to lax hiring standards, even for rookies, as an additional factor explaining some instances of police brutality or abuse. Consequently, law enforcement leaders must more assertively cull from their forces individuals who turn out to be unsuited to serve. This will not be easy. Stepping over this "blue line" requires courage, tenacity, and the surmounting of legal and bureaucratic obstacles erected over decades. But it is nothing less than imperative.

There are some ways law enforcement leaders can implement effective change. I believe that the amplified use of employee assistance programs can be an essential aid as we address potential problems, reassignments, transfers, and separations. This, too, can help ensure that we have the best people on the street serving the public. As I also wrote in that *Times-Union* column:

> *These "bad" officers have a license to kill. It is in the best interest of all involved that we remove these officers who could be a threat. That could mean reassignment, transfer, or separation from law enforcement service. There is no process or concession that should…allow a person to wear a badge and gun in our community to enforce laws if that person is unsuited for the position.*

Rank-and-file police officers can identify rogue cops, but no one desires to be perceived as an informant or snitch. These true professionals must be convinced that it is in their best interest to rid their departments of officers who tarnish the badge. Sheriffs, police chiefs, and their entire leadership teams must step up, but things become far more complicated here.

For one thing, these leaders must remain mindful of the overall morale of their departments. Where are those lines between being sufficiently aggressive in cleansing their forces and being overly aggressive to the point of undermining the morale and unity of those forces? Even when that dicey course is navigated, it brings law enforcement leaders to the perilous and growing obstacles constructed by police unions.

A comprehensive study by the *New York Times* published in December 2020 found that decades of initiatives led by police unions erected enormous and often unassailable obstacles to the removal or significant disciplining of rogue cops. Police contracts. Court cases. Arbitration decisions. According to the study, all these things contributed to shielding officers from scrutiny. One instructive excerpt reads:

> While the Black Lives Matter protests this year have aimed to address police violence against people of color, another wave of protests a half-century ago was exploited to gain the protections that now often allow officers accused of excessive force to avoid discipline.
>
> That effort took off in Detroit, partly as a backlash to the civil rights movement of the 1960s when police officers around the country—who at times acted as instruments of suppression for political officials or were accused of brutality in quelling unrest—felt vulnerable to citizen complaints.

Newly formed police unions leveraged fears of lawlessness and an era of high crime to win disciplinary constraints, often far beyond those of other public employees. Over fifty years, these protections, expanded in contracts and laws, have built a robust system for law enforcement officers. As a result, critics said, officers empowered to protect the public were instead protected from the public. Most disciplinary cases against officers now go to arbitration. And these arbitrators, glancing backward at union contracts and recently established precedents, rule about half the time in favor of accused officers. "Some arbitrators referred to termination as 'economic capital punishment' or 'economic murder,'" the *Times* reported. Worse, even well-intended efforts to reform systems of monitoring, investigating, and punishing rogue cops often fail to bear fruit. In 2015, then New York governor Andrew Cuomo ordered those cases involving police killings of unarmed suspects be investigated by the state's attorney general rather than local prosecutors with close ties to those same police officers. The interim result? More than five years later, none of the first forty-three such investigations led to a conviction.

So that's where we are now—with police chiefs and sheriffs, mayors, and city commissioners often finding themselves powerless to rid their forces of problem officers. In response, law enforcement leaders must be sufficiently courageous and creative to take on police unions and other collective bargaining units that protect questionable officers. A rogue police officer holds power and authority too deadly to perpetuate within the framework of collective bargaining protection.

In recent years, some states have attempted to deal with these issues, though few have taken all the necessary steps. In my home state of Florida, no-knock warrants have been prohibited, and the legislature passed, and the governor signed in June 2021, police reform legislation that can be seen as a good start. It mandates certain use-of-force policies, including training on de-escalation techniques. It requires officers to intervene if they see excessive force being employed by a colleague. Importantly, it also requires that disciplinary records follow an officer when they leave one department and apply for employment at another. But it does not go far enough. Among other things, though it discourages choke holds, it does not ban them. These are challenges, but we've met and overcome criminal justice challenges before.

Remember the controversy over "Miranda rights," the obligation imposed on police by the US Supreme Court in 1966 to inform criminal suspects in custody of their right to remain silent? "You have the right to remain silent. Anything you say can and will be used against you in a court of law. You have the right to talk to a lawyer for advice before we ask you any questions. You have the right to have a lawyer with you during questioning. If you cannot afford a lawyer, one will be appointed for you." Well, many thought we'd never get another confession. They were wrong. Reading suspects their Miranda rights made confessions and other information shared by suspects more solid and more usable in court.

I am convinced that law enforcement as a profession is better off by having implemented those rights for suspects.

CHAPTER 15

RUNNING FOR MAYOR: BATTLING TWO OPPONENTS AND UGLY SLURS

Honor in defeat, and I passed the baton to another.

From time to time, I harbor the thought that maybe I shouldn't be quite so driven. Maybe it's OK, every now and then, to reject that latest kernel of devotion and ambition that propels me to embrace a new, once-unimagined challenge. Hasn't happened yet, but …

After serving for eight years as sheriff, the path seemed clear for reelection to another four-year term, given that term limits on this job had recently been lifted by the courts. One of my closest cabinet members, Director of Corrections John Rutherford, had been quietly considering a challenge, but Under sheriff John Gordon had a word with him, and Rutherford decided to stand down until the next opportunity. So I was looking at the luxury of an unopposed third term during the election of April 15, 2003. That would truly cement the historic nature of what my supporters and I already had accomplished in once white-dominated Jacksonville, Florida. But I tend toward self-awareness and self-analysis, and I knew at a deep level that the spark was flickering. I had lost some of my zeal and enthusiasm for the job. Eight years—nearly three thousand days—as sheriff of a growing, diverse, politically tense, and economically stratified metropolitan area can take a lot out of anyone.

The pressure was unrelenting, and it often came from all sides. But my public approval ratings were extremely high—averaging in the 75 percent range—and many people already had come to me, suggesting I run to succeed Mayor John Delaney, a Republican with whom I had an excellent relationship and who was stepping down due to term limits. This would be another, once-inconceivable concept. No African American previously had staged a viable campaign for mayor of Jacksonville, much less served in that position. I sensed the same dynamic happening that had propelled me into running for sheriff: when somebody injects a thought into my mind, I find it hard to resist. I don't ever want to look back and think I rejected an opportunity or a challenge due to fear of failure. That dynamic, plus the sheer opportunity to make history and do good, proved compelling and irresistible. Steve and Gary Pajcic adopted the same position they had taken when I was thinking about running for sheriff: they told me that if I decided to run, this time for mayor, they would help me. "Let's do it!" I said.

At that time in Jacksonville, the system worked like this: candidates for most elected city positions competed in an April election. If no one achieved at least 50 percent plus one vote, the top two finishers competed again in a May runoff. Technically, these were nonpartisan elections, but everyone knew which candidates were Democrats and which were Republicans.

The resulting mayoral campaign paralleled, to a great degree, my initial run for sheriff. Many in the city saw it as an uphill battle, but they believed I was not only capable of handling the job, they thought I had the perfect combination of administrative, political, and public communications skills for the position. Still, many others didn't see it that way. They thought that others in the race were more qualified. That's fine. It's the way it works here in the United States.

We campaigned hard and felt good about our effort. But we faced two significant challenges. Seven people ended up qualifying for the race: three Democrats and four Republicans. It would be virtually impossible for anyone to capture more than half of the total vote. One of those seven was another African American, Betty Holzendorf, a former state senator with whom I had a bit of a history and whose radio ads focused their attacks primarily on me rather than on the Republicans who were running. Also a graduate of Edward Waters College, Betty entered the race late, just a few days before the deadline, and proved to be a somewhat divisive figure. Frankly, this was not helpful to my campaign. Nevertheless, I decided to take the high road, avoiding counterattacks and really, any attacks on my opponents.

One of the highlights of the campaign was a televised debate on WJXT, News4JAX. With seven candidates on the stage, only a handful of questions could be asked, and therefore just a few issues were addressed, but one of those issues was race and how I would handle it:

First thing, the mayor should take a leadership role in that. I welcome taking that role. One of the problems, called a race problem in the city, is a lack of trust. And a lot of that has to do with the past. We still have a generation here who will not let go of the past.

Now, things are getting better. Things are not where they should be, but thank God they are not where they were at one time. We need to continue communication. We need to continue working with each other. And I think we've had a mayor who closed that gap significantly over the last eight years. And I'm just proud to have been a part of that. And I would like to see us continue that goodwill. But it's going to take a mayor with the courage and a desire to solve this problem of racism, and I think we can do a better job at it. And I'm committed to doing just that…

I've walked every neighborhood in this city. I talked to the people across their fences, on their lawns, in their neighborhoods, and in their living rooms. And the people have told me what they want. I've … touched the people. I feel the people. I know what they want. I'll do the same thing as mayor. I will take government to the people. I do want this community's vote. I want their help, but most of all, I want their prayers.

My campaign worked, and with 27.96 percent of the vote, I won the first election, which essentially became a primary since none of us secured 50 percent plus one of the votes. Second place went to John Peyton, a white Republican who snagged 23.66 percent of the vote, and Betty Holzendorf received 2.42 percent of the vote.

John Peyton and I faced off a month later in the runoff. John was a wealthy businessman backed by his family's real estate, fuel station, and convenience store fortune. His campaign was very well-financed. Though I had the resources I needed, it felt like a David and Goliath campaign.

Campaigning this time around was quite different than when I ran for sheriff. Seeds of division had been sown. There was campaign rhetoric, which had taken place during the primaries, that had chilled the enthusiasm of the voter base, significantly contributing to a great degree of voter apathy. The Deep South reared its ugly head again.

Election Night

The Glover family on election night, April 11, 1995, the night Nathaniel Glover was elected the first Black sheriff in Jacksonville, Florida. Pictured are his wife, son, and daughter. *<Photo courtesy of David Williams.>*

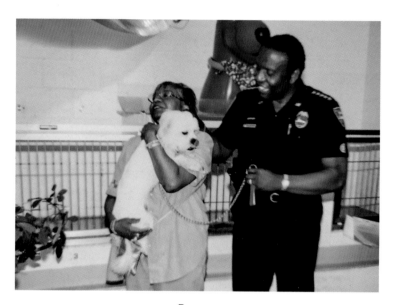

Roscoe

Nat and his wife, Doris, at the Jacksonville Humane Society, where they adopted their dog, Roscoe. Roscoe was part of the Glover family for nearly fifteen years.

Hall of Fame

Nat Glover is inducted into the Florida Law Enforcement Officers' Hall of Fame. He is joined by (from left to right): Lauralyn Glover (Nat's son's wife); Michael Glover (Nat's son); Doris Glover (Nat's wife); Dr. David W. Green, Sr. Pastor of Saint Stephen AME Church (Nat's pastor); Nathaniel Glover; Clemantine Glover (Nat's daughter); Shirley Williams (Nat's sister); and Charles Williams (Nat's brother-in-law).

Mom & Dad

Mom and Dad Glover, Arsie B. and Nathaniel, on Stewart Street after leaving church services at New Mt. Pleasant Baptist Church in Jacksonville, Florida.

Nat, in Office

Sheriff Nat Glover in his office as he signs an autograph, which he
did regularly during his time as sheriff and still does to this day.

Dr. Nathaniel Glover Receives Rotary Club's Paul Harris Fellow Recognition

President Dr. Nat Glover

President of Edward Waters College, Nat Glover, in a photo taken upon his receipt of the Rotary Club's Paul Harris Fellow recognition.

Shotgun House

Newly elected Sheriff Nat Glover standing on the land where his childhood home once stood at 734 Minnie Street, Jacksonville, Florida. The house in the picture is his neighbor's home, whose construction is the same shotgun style as his former home.

Football

Young Nat Glover in his Edward Waters
College (now University) football team
uniform. He was captain of his team
during his junior and senior years.

Someone spray-painted "NO NIGGER MAYOR" on the outside wall of my campaign headquarters. The words "NIGGER LOVER" were sprayed on a sign outside the insurance office of Matt Carlucci, a white Republican who had been an opponent during the primary election but who now supported me.

Carlucci's support didn't come without repercussion to him. It was an extremely courageous act during these times of racial divide. Yet he backed me, adding fuel to the racial fire, which had never been fully extinguished. If being sheriff was like being the quarterback on a football team and being mayor was like being the coach, it would seem that Jacksonville had the appetite for a Black quarterback but not a Black coach.

My campaign ended up making national news. A report was broadcast on Anderson Cooper's CNN program, wire services transmitted coverage around the world, and major newspapers dispatched correspondents to town. At one point, we released what CNN called a "searing radio attack ad" in which we called out Peyton for promising to fire a Black fire chief and eliminating some minority city contracts.

"If John Peyton is mayor," I said in that ad, "Jacksonville will turn back the clock on community relations."

Peyton's campaign fired back, attacking my record as sheriff, saying, "Several rogue officers he hired were convicted of murder, robbery, and other crimes."

It all became a hugely disappointing and contentious situation. Eventually, both Peyton and I denounced the racist graffiti, and Peyton contributed to a $25,000 reward fund for the capture of the perpetrators. Still, some of his supporters began a whisper campaign, an absurd effort that accused us of staging the controversy in an effort to damage Peyton and win sympathy. Despite our best efforts and all the progress Jacksonville had made, race and racism were factors in our city again. As Matthew Corrigan, a political science professor at the University of

North Florida, told a TV reporter, "Race is always in the background. In the South, you won't find an election without race being a factor.

As the May 13, 2003, runoff election approached, things were not looking good for us. We encountered indifference in the Black community—indifference that was aggravated and instigated by some of the political players from the primary. That, plus John Peyton's genuine popularity, were insurmountable obstacles. Peyton ended up winning the election with 58 percent of the vote. I received 96,714 votes to his 133,554 votes. Though my supporters seemed crushed, I did not feel depressed or monumentally disappointed. I believe the people always get it right (well, almost always). I consistently have believed that there can be much honor in defeat and that triumph comes from being willing to run a race, not necessarily placing first or even crossing the finish line.

Nonetheless, the election remained historic. As an African American man in a runoff race for mayor of Jacksonville, Florida, I had destroyed another backward tradition in the Deep South, and many people give me credit for having paved the path for the eventual first Black mayor of Jacksonville, Alvin Brown, and other high local posts that soon were occupied by Black people. In fact, Alvin Brown himself, on many occasions, has given me credit for his election, and I'm proud of that. Once again, African Americans who had been striving for justice were making important inroads in the Deep South.

I felt like I had lost gracefully and was confident I could hold my head high. As a matter of fact, people were still treating me like a hero. In my concession speech on election night, I congratulated John and pledged to assist him as he took office. Little did I know what that would soon entail. Losing the race catapulted me toward my life's next journey, which truly was impactful, and I realized the extent to which unintended consequences can prove incredibly beneficial and satisfying. I believe to this day that my unsuccessful run for mayor gave me an even greater opportunity to make a difference.

CHAPTER 16

TWO TRANSITIONS AND THE JACKSONVILLE COMMITMENT

We kept at-risk kids in college. We made a difference.

Within a day or two of my loss at the polls, I received a call from Mayor-Elect John Peyton. To my astonishment, he asked me—his defeated rival in an extremely contentious and racially tinged election —to join his team and serve as co-chair of his transition. That was virtually unprecedented. I had never heard of an opposing candidate serving on the victor's transition team, especially as co-chair. Sure, I had said in my concession speech that I wanted us to come together, but. . . come on. That was intended mostly in the philosophical sense. I never envisioned literally working with him. But here he was, the incoming mayor, a wealthy white Republican, only the second Republican elected as Jacksonville's mayor since 1888, seeking my help.

Here's what John said to explain this highly unusual move, which was one of the most courageous acts I have ever seen:

We need to first understand the circumstances in 2003. The sheriff was my opponent in the general election, and he ran a formidable, highly respected campaign with significant support from the minority community—about 30 percent of the electorate.

The sheriff and I already had a good relationship that stretched from before the campaign. Although I won 58 percent of the vote, it was very lopsided. I did not have the support of our African American community, and I was concerned about the potential impact of festering racial issues and a lack of community trust.

All our community needed to have a voice. I knew we had to come together as a community. Heal as a community. Move forward together rather than apart. But we both had supporters that were highly invested and extremely vocal. Some of my backers felt we had won; we had a platform, and now we could not "give in." But this was no longer a campaign, and as mayor, I served the whole of the Jacksonville community.

I knew the skills and tools used for the campaign were very different from those you would use for governing. There was only one person I knew who could help to bridge the divide—Sheriff Glover. The sheriff had had a very successful law enforcement career, including a focus on community policing, and he understood government.

Inviting the sheriff to be part of the solution for our community was a natural next step. I called him and made my request for him to co-chair my administration's transition team. I remember hearing silence—he clearly thought it was maybe a joke.

It certainly was not a joke, and by reading John's words, you understand his empathetic, generous character. Furthermore, I understood where he was coming from. When I was elected sheriff, I also reached out to my opponent's supporters as I built my top staff.

I think it's important here and for the historical record to add a bit more background because it demonstrates how committed much of the white leadership of Jacksonville was, at the turn of the twenty-first century, to finding a new path toward racial understanding and equity. You'd have to search far to find a more core member of the white establishment at that time than Walt Bussell, chief executive officer of the city-owned Jacksonville Electric Authority, the only power utility in town. He served the JEA for nearly three full decades, and he remains widely respected to this day as a community leader.

Walt was one of my closest advisers, and he had agreed to chair my transition committee if I won the election. Now he was chairing John's transition committee. It all was a little head-spinning. John has made it clear that what was top of mind for him was to unify the city. He didn't feel the need to acquiesce to some of his advisers. He wanted to effectively govern the city and put politics aside. To this day, he says he feels like it was "the best decision" of his administration. Here, in Walt's words, is how it happened:

> I knew Nat for over fifteen years. I was the CEO of JEA when he was the sheriff. We worked closely together on a number of initiatives. When Nat ran for mayor, we had a discussion that I would help with his transition.
>
> Nevertheless, I received a call from Herb Peyton, John Peyton's old-fashioned father, who asked if I would have coffee with his eldest son, John. We met at Starbucks in Five Points, a historical part of Jacksonville on the periphery of downtown.

*I reiterated to John that I was supporting Nat. John said he
was a novice in the government field and asked if I would support
his transition team if he won. He further said that if he won, he
wanted to focus on reaching out and working together with the
sheriff. He believed Nat was a formidable candidate. He was sincere.
No Republicans, no Democrats, but a team focused on supporting
Jacksonville was his goal.*

*Later, his sincere desire for overall unity resulted in his supporters
feeling he was abandoning his party by bringing the "other side" into
his administration and transition team. John's risky collaborative
perspective did cause issues—some of his most staunch supporters
picketed his mayoral offices.*

As John and Walt suggested, some of John's campaign donors were
not happy about his extension of a hand of fellowship to me, but his
professional team overruled those donors and were unanimously in
favor of bringing me aboard, according to Kerri Stewart, one of his top
aides, who recalls: "I was in the room when a lot of the decisions were
made. All the consultants for the transition team thought it would be a
great idea to provide the necessary support to bring the community back
together. I believe this was the start of a friendship between the mayor
and sheriff that has lasted until this day."

She believes correctly. It was, as they now say, a no-brainer. I was
touched and honored to co-chair John's transition team, and we have
remained close ever since. Our working relationship and friendship
endured even after John was solidly in place at the mayor's office. Making
the decision to work as part of John's transition team was fairly easy for
me because my mindset was solely focused on finding ways to make the
lives of Jacksonville's citizens easier and safer.

Once the transition was completed, John and I continued to meet
regularly to discuss and work on an increasingly vexing problem, among

other challenges. The city was beginning to experience a significant spike in crime. Though I had been succeeded as sheriff by the very capable John Rutherford, and fighting crime was his primary responsibility, it seemed obvious that I might be of assistance to the mayor. I made clear to John that he could not "bigfoot" the sheriff by trying to do his job but that we could deploy a strategy I had used when I was sheriff—what I called the "advisory council model." This new council, which would include a diverse assembly of some of the most prominent people in town, would address not only criminal activity but also its root causes and then suggest solutions that could lead to additional resources for the sheriff's office.

Importantly, I made certain to meet with Sheriff Rutherford and keep him updated on the creation and progress of this initiative. One of my foremost philosophies in life: widen the circle of those invested in your plan and, whenever possible, show them how they might benefit from it.

Here, again, is what former mayor Peyton said:

> There were two definitive issues we needed to tackle almost immediately. We saw a significant spike in crime but no definitive answers as to who would be responsible for the problems. Historically, JSO owned the crime problem in the form of enforcement, but it was becoming evident to me that the magnitude of the problem was more than an enforcement issue. The cycle of violence had deeper layers.
>
> Sheriff Glover is renowned for bringing people together to provide reasonable options. With his help, my administration launched a major participatory team—120 people from every critical sector of our community.
>
> Many of the members were not necessarily directly connected to the prime issues, but bringing a wide group of diverse people together was the key. We created a tremendous work product. A three-legged stool was created: enforcement, prevention, and intervention.

The program would require a lot of money and political capital. Many of the members had the political capital to engage the city council, which had not allocated funds in the past.

There was a risk of stepping on toes with JSO and the super- intendent of schools. The superintendent had put troubled students

The long fight against violent crime

Mayor John Peyton formed the Jacksonville Journey in 2007 to "reverse the tide of violence" that made Duval County the murder capital of Florida. The county's murder rate dropped significantly for several years, but it is rising again. Figures are for murders per 100,000 residents to account for population growth during the past decade.

Murder rate per 100,000 residents in Duval County
[Actual number of murders]

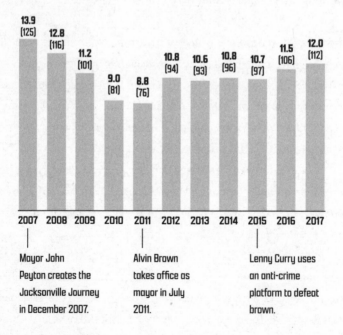

on the street—we needed his assistance in strengthening crime-prevention programs.

This entire $31-million-per-year program had a tremendous impact. My administration's mantra was paying it forward, collaborative leadership, trust, and authenticity, and this allowed us to achieve some great results.

Basically, the initiative had two main components: Rally Jacksonville, a program that concentrated on literacy and other educational efforts, and the Jacksonville Journey, a $31 million package of crime prevention and intervention initiatives. I was involved with both, although I tended to focus mostly on the Jacksonville Journey. The results were truly phenomenal. We experienced a consistent decline in crime between 2007–2011. It is one of my proudest collaborations. The chart on page 194 demonstrates the sharp reductions in the murder and other violent crime rates.

Simultaneously, we launched another, even more sweeping initiative that we called the Jacksonville Commitment. What did Jacksonville commit to? Assisting every willing but underprivileged high school graduate in our county to attend a local university or college. Everyone. Period. This was the outgrowth of my lengthy law enforcement career, and it was triggered by a confrontation of sorts with a woman who seemed to have been sent by an angel.

As an insider, I had been a displeased observer of the racial and other disparities in our criminal justice system. I'm a realist, and I knew that the entire system could not be changed and improved in one fell swoop, but I also knew that people can make subtle and impactful changes of good faith. And that makes sense on every level, even economically. Studies show that state after state regularly spends more each year to imprison someone than it would cost to send that same person to an elite Ivy League university. And, of course, a college education significantly enhances a person's lifetime earning power, almost doubling it over that of a high school graduate. So providing our most socially disenfranchised youth with another, better option remains my passion, but it also should be society's passion. We can and must reduce the number of young people going to jail, diverting them to college instead, one person at a time. This is another instance where education is truly transformational, with the power to change life trajectories.

Even though, as a "retiree," I was assisting Mayor Peyton with his anti-crime efforts, I have to admit that I was becoming a little complacent, a little too relaxed. But then, someone again was put in my path to nudge me in the right direction.

A woman I did not know and never saw again stopped me on the street one Friday evening and insisted on engaging me in a difficult conversation. She simply would not let me go. She was concerned about what was happening on the streets of Jacksonville—that so many young people were dying in the city, in our city. She found it unfathomable that I was not more visibly and actively engaged in dealing with this. She also said God had given me the ability and the knowledge to deal with this type of situation, and I was squandering those talents. Tears fell from her eyes as she blamed me for much of this terrible situation: "How can you sit around and see people dying and not help us?" She came like a prophet, reminding me of what God had given me, what was true, and what was at stake if I remained complacent. I politely acknowledged her concerns and extricated myself, but it was not over. I could not sleep that night. That woman had shaken me, awakened me. I sat on the edge of my bed, gazing at the clock, watching the minutes tick by.

I just had to speak with someone who understood my situation and now my dilemma. That someone I knew was John Delaney, who had served as mayor when I was sheriff and now served as the influential president of the University of North Florida (UNF), our largest local college and part of the state university system. Though from different parties, John (a Republican) and I (a Democrat) had an excellent relationship. When he served as mayor and I served as sheriff, politics never entered into our work or discussions. We both were committed to doing what we thought best for our community. Occasionally, he would ask me to include something important to him in my budget, and he helped me achieve several major building projects. We did all of this without hesitation or reservation. So I waited until what I considered a respectable time on a Saturday morning to call John. I wanted to ensure he was at least out of bed. By nine o'clock, I could not wait any longer.

I told John about the confrontation with the woman. He said he had not had a similar experience but would like to meet with me. He said his father had advised him to contact me about providing assistance at UNF. I had always told John that his father was also one of those angels I believed had been sent to lead me in the right direction at crucial junctures of my life. This was one of those moments in time. It would be difficult to overstate the significance of that meeting with John Delaney. It launched a whole new odyssey—a crusade to educate our youth.

The Jacksonville Commitment was conceived—a commitment to help our underprivileged students earn a college degree to break the cycle of poverty and crime that the woman I had encountered complained about. But how to accomplish this? We looked around the country for a model and found a program called the Kalamazoo Promise. It had been created in 2005 by anonymous local donors who agreed to fund four years of tuition in any Michigan public college or university for every qualified graduate of Kalamazoo's public schools. Thousands of students were able to take advantage of this program, graduating with college degrees at virtually no cost to them. We modeled the Jacksonville Commitment on the Kalamazoo program. I was appointed as special assistant to UNF president Delaney, which was a cabinet-level position, and I was called "Jacksonville's Ambassador for Higher Education."

As part of the program, which began in 2007, we enlisted Duval County Public Schools, the City of Jacksonville, and all four institutions of higher learning in Jacksonville: UNF; my HBCU alma mater, Edward Waters College; Florida State College Jacksonville (FSCJ); and the private Jacksonville University.

In announcing the program, Delaney noted that I was the beneficiary of local college programs and already had striven to pay it forward. "As further evidence of his passion for higher education," Delaney told the gathered media, "you'll remember that Nat has donated his own pension benefits, worth nearly a quarter of a million dollars, to a scholarship fund for low-income children."

This was a reference to the Nat Glover Scholars program, one of the most satisfying things I've ever done that can be attributed to the great influence of the Pajcic brothers. I wanted to emulate their philanthropist mindset. Christopher Conway, one of the first beneficiaries of my scholar's fund, wrote to me: "This scholarship has helped me strive to do my best in academic areas, as well as in discipline. Without this program, I would not be able to fulfill my dreams of becoming a firefighter. Now I have the opportunity to further my education and give back to the community."

Imagine that—a young man from the ghetto, following his dream to serve the public. And I was in a position to assist him. I felt great pride for being able to pay it forward, grateful that I could serve in this way, and hopeful for Chris and all the Nat Glover scholars. Just as importantly, I felt introspective about my journey, my eyes wide-open to seeing the blessings bestowed upon me throughout my life.

To move the Jacksonville Commitment forward, we identified young people who, due to their economic status, were eligible for maximum federal government Pell Grants to be used for education. Each student had to meet minimum entrance standards. They could select any major they desired. We realized that socioeconomic disadvantages could inhibit their success in college, so we raised funds to provide a full menu of counseling, tutoring, and other support services, along with additional scholarships as needed. The city contributed $1 million, and other donors pitched in. Any remaining financial gaps were absorbed by the colleges and universities.

This holistic program considered the impediments that often cause students to drop out. It's such an echo of my brother's, Eugene's, and my initial experiences in college. It was intended to be an answer to the challenges we both faced and to give the kind of support that keeps a student in school. Plus, in this program, a student wouldn't have to be a phenomenal athlete in order to gain entrance to university.

"If Jacksonville is going to prosper," I said. "we must ensure that our citizens are well educated. Too many high school students don't think a college degree is possible because of the cost. The Jacksonville Commitment is our way, the community's way, of eliminating the cost barrier."

Dr. Ouida Powe, who served as director of the Jacksonville Commitment, put it this way:

> The bundling with academic advisement was not new. There were many similar programs nationwide. The difference with the Jacksonville Commitment was the strong governance structure. Sheriff Glover was able to bring the right people together to make the program a success. At the beginning of the program, we had the right executives on board, who were very committed to the program.

As a result, graduation rates for at-risk students were about 10 to 15 percent higher than for other student cohorts. The successes were so significant that we discussed offering these services to the entire high school student body. Between 2008 and 2014, the Jacksonville Commitment helped 948 local high school graduates attend participating colleges.

Their accomplishments were noteworthy. One interned at NASA and invented a device that flew on the space shuttle. All eight who later applied to law school were accepted. Many expressed their gratitude for the life-changing opportunities afforded to them by the program.

DeSean Kirkland, who was raised in low-income housing by his mother and whose father had been murdered, became a recipient of the first Jacksonville Commitment award and went on to become a music major at UNF. "Thank God for the Jacksonville Commitment," he told the *Jacksonville Times-Union.* "All I knew [about] was loans and debt. I associated college with loans, hardship, struggle, and debt. I wasn't going to go to school, is what I'm saying. If it had not been for this. College gives parents an opportunity to be proud of their children. It gives children an opportunity to make their parents proud." DeSean was not alone. We kept a number of high-risk kids in college.

Sadly, however, after seven years of success, the program died in 2015, along with the more controversial Jacksonville Journey anti-crime initiative, after Mayor Peyton left office. Some may not acknowledge this, but every four to eight years, the price of democracy is paid. New administrations have their own agendas and are not committed to carrying forward the policies, practices, or programs of those in office before them. Therefore, our program was the victim of politics.

"It became a political hot potato," Dr. Powe recalls. "Some of the key members of the committee started to establish their own programs, and we lost overall momentum as a city. There were several fumbles, egos, and a lack of cohesive unity. In the end, our regional youth suffered."

Indeed, they did. To this day, one of my dreams is to resurrect the Jacksonville Commitment.

Personally, having a cabinet-level seat at UNF served as an introduction to higher education management—an education I didn't know I would soon need. There I was, listening and learning about the nuts and bolts of academic administration and leadership, the concerns and crises, responses, and solutions. In essence, I received an advanced degree in higher education leadership—one that served me well for my eventual return to Edward Waters College.

My tenure at UNF emerged as one of my greatest life blessings. These days, they call it paying it forward. I call it doing good and helping my fellow man and woman. Can anything be more satisfying, especially if it involves elevating members of a younger generation?

CHAPTER 17

PRESIDENT NAT GLOVER: REINVIGORATING MY COLLEGE ALMA MATER

The condition of the campus was appalling.

For years as a student, I cleaned college restrooms virtually every day. Now I was sitting in the president's office. My office. It was an unbelievable, inconceivable turn of events. After decades of public service, seven years of retirement—or maybe, more accurately, semiretirement—at the age of sixty-seven, I was now president of Edward Waters College (EWC), my alma mater.

In 2003, the voters of Jacksonville had metaphorically signed my retirement papers. In 2010, I agreed to serve as interim—and ultimately permanent—president of Edward Waters College and its eight hundred–member student body. The role for which I unknowingly had spent a lifetime preparing was thrust upon me. And it was a hell of a challenge.

Edward Waters was—and still is—deeply associated with the African Methodist Episcopal (AME) Church. At one point in history, to serve Black students who had few other opportunities to achieve higher education, the AME church supported twenty-eight colleges and seminaries, the first established in 1856. Today, with minorities achieving at least some equity in college admissions, the church helps support six colleges (including Edward Waters) and two seminaries. And that support remains significant. About one-third of the denomination's entire budget goes to higher education.

That support certainly was and is appreciated, but the truth is that the college I loved, the institution that propelled me into a life of service and accomplishment, the place that, in many ways, had saved my life, was tottering. A series of less-than-ideal Edward Waters presidents, appointed by a well-meaning board dominated by well-meaning African Methodist Episcopal Church officials, had unintentionally inflicted significant damage.

EWC teetered on the brink of financial collapse, and it faced total ruin. Most ominously, EWC again was in danger of losing its accreditation, a truly existential threat. Had that happened, we likely would have had to close the doors and send our students, teachers, and administrators packing. In 2004, six years before I took over, EWC sent what turned out to be partially plagiarized recertification documents to the Commission on Colleges of the Southern Association of Colleges and Schools (SACSCOC). One of those documents referred to our "rolling hills," of which we have none. That text and some statistics apparently were copied from documents previously submitted by Alabama A&M University.

SACSCOC voted to revoke Edward Waters's accreditation in response, potentially a death blow. The school lost an appeal at

SACSCOC but won an injunction from a federal court. Ultimately, EWC was allowed to resubmit its application and was reaccredited in 2006. But the school was alerted and told, "We're watching you. Don't mess up again, and make sure that your required five-year update is perfect." But … it wasn't.

That five-year report was due shortly after I came in as interim president. Not knowing very much about this, I didn't ask the right questions. We failed. The report was inadequate. Our liaison at SACSCOC said, "This is not good enough. You are back on warning."

So we were again in the crosshairs of the SACSCOC, and I had a major crisis on my hands: dealing with another erosion of our public perception and our credibility. The community said, "Here we go again." It was awful.

Then the crisis deepened when my executive vice president resigned, forcing me to fill that position at such a critical time. It's hard to believe what happened next, but it again illustrates the force—I believe it is divine—that has continually placed the right people in my path at the right time.

We advertised the position of executive vice president and narrowed the applicants to three who would be interviewed by a small selection team and me. Mostly, I was looking for someone who had significant experience with SACSCOC accreditation because that was the first fire I had to extinguish. This was a remote Skype interview process so I placed the top three candidates' folders on my desk. Folders for the others whom I had rejected were stored on a shelf under my desk. When I entered the office the next day, a fourth folder was on my desk. I figured my executive assistant had placed it there for some reason, so I didn't think very much about it as I returned it to the lower shelf. The next day, the same thing happened—the same fourth folder was back on my desk. Then it happened a third time. At that point, I looked at this folder more closely, liked what I saw, and thought, *Fine. Let's interview her too.*

That application had come from Anna Hammond, a former academic affairs officer at Edward Waters, and she blew us away. She had just left Mississippi Valley State University, and—bingo! —had led the team there that earned reaccreditation. This was not stated on her application explicitly enough to get my attention, but it came out in the interview. We hired her, and she did an excellent job leading the team of professionals responsible for meeting the requirements for reaffirmation of accreditation for the institution. We satisfied the folks at SACSCOC. Anna Hammond's folder shouldn't have been on my desk, yet it was— persistently. I like to think that was divine intervention.

⚖

I didn't set out to be the president of Edward Waters College. My goal was to recruit a stellar candidate for the role, but an indomitable bishop had other plans. In February 2010, after just a little more than two years in the position, EWC president Dr. Claudette Williams abruptly resigned. This was the last thing the endangered institution needed, and it deeply worried the EWC board of trustees, chaired by Senior Bishop McKinley Young of the African Methodist Episcopal Church, which remained closely associated with EWC.

Within what seemed like nanoseconds of learning of the presidential vacancy, Bishop Young called me and asked for assistance. I had learned that when Bishop Young reached out, you had better respond. Born and raised in Atlanta, the holder of three college degrees and six honorary degrees, Bishop Young had been pastor of numerous AME churches, and he served in countless other ecumenical, educational, and civic roles. He was an impressive, highly admired man, and his passing in January 2019 was a great loss to all. Bishop Young's initial request was that I try to persuade Adam Herbert to assume the position of interim president at Edward Waters College. Doctor Herbert was an African American and former president of the University of North Florida, former chancellor of Florida's entire state university system, and former president of Indiana University. Adam was the perfect candidate for this tough role.

As a board member, I strongly supported this plan and decided to enlist UNF president John Delaney in the effort. I briefed John about EWC's dilemma and the board's plan to recruit Adam as interim president. John agreed to accompany me to a meeting with Adam, but he swiftly added that I should consider shouldering the EWC challenge. I knew that people would take him seriously, and I really did not embrace this idea. "John," I said, "do not say that to anyone else. Promise me." He reluctantly agreed.

We began trying to schedule a meeting with Adam, but other plans were bubbling under the surface, and the meeting never took place. It turns out that when John looked at his cell phone a little later that day, he found a series of attempted calls from Ava Parker, general counsel for the Eleventh Episcopal District of the AME Church. She had urged Bishop Young, and now she was urging John Delaney, to press me into service as EWC's interim president. With her knowledge and expertise about the type of academic leadership and oversight it would take to act as president of a college, I was pleasantly surprised to find out that she believed I was the right person for the job. While I had all the necessary qualities to get the job done, I believed that EWC needed someone with an impeccable educational background—someone with a PhD or EdD But everyone else believed differently.

I received a call directly from Bishop Young urging me to consider taking on the role of interim president. I recall telling him I appreciated his confidence in me, but I did not believe I was the right person for the position. I did not have a doctoral degree, and without all the commonly accepted credentials, I did not believe I would enjoy community support. A Who's Who of community leaders, including my former mayoral opponent Betty Holzendorf, soon gathered in the bishop's office, and they placed a call to me as I was on the way to Tampa for a meeting. Bishop Young said the community leaders were in his office at that very moment. He put me on speakerphone, and they went around the table. Each person reiterated their resolute support for my becoming the interim president of EWC. And they all emphasized that I should accept.

Bishop Young was a formidable man. I relented and agreed to take the interim position beginning in May 2010. As I think of it now, God orchestrated my path accordingly and prepared me for such a time and such a need.

Edward Waters College was plagued with crises. There was the previous accreditation issue, which I've already discussed. But there were also many situations that needed to be resolved, and I didn't really know which way to turn. I remember thinking, *What am I facing, and how should we respond?* Our graduation rate was just 15 percent—that's how many of our entering freshmen managed to graduate, compared to 41 percent at both Florida A&M and Bethune-Cookman, our nearby HBCUs. We absolutely had to do better. We had an open enrollment policy, meaning anyone who made it through high school could attend EWC, but many students were not ready for college. Too many of them just dropped out, never to return. Other students ended up transferring elsewhere. When students didn't return, their tuition payments didn't return. And less tuition further burdened our already tenuous budget. As a result, the board of trustees, of which I was a past member, passed a mandate that required students to have a 2.5 grade point average for admission to Edward Waters College. To be honest, I was somewhat reluctant to vote for it because I thought it might be inconsistent with the school's mission. I also questioned if I would have met those admissions requirements when I was planning to attend Edward Waters. But I later voted for the mandate, and it passed the board unanimously.

Admission standards for most American colleges and universities have consistently allowed a minimum of 10 percent of the entering freshman classes to be admitted with less than the required high school grade point average. This practice is used to address issues of diversity and inclusion (special admissions policies). During my administration, the Office of Admissions published information that indicated that the GPA of the classes entering Edward Waters College was trending upward. The Office of the Registrar verified that the number of students admitted under the special admissions policy was consistently less than 5 percent of each class. We never got close to the 10 percent special admission policy threshold. Our commitment to addressing the trustee board mandate for higher GPAs for entering students was fulfilled.

By the time I turned the job over to Dr. A. Zachary Faison Jr. in 2017, we had continued to mandate a 2.5 high school grade point average, and our graduation rate rose to 31.9 percent—better than it had been, although we still had a long way to go when it came to freshman retention and the six-year graduation rate.

At the same time, our faculty and staff had been shaken by layoffs, diminished resources, and a general sense of malaise. They wanted to talk, so we did. I told them that I had to assess the entire situation, and we all had to straighten out the business end of the equation, and then we would get back on track. And we did. I looked at the hiring process, contracts, human resources, and every facet of the college's operations. We collegially instituted improvements across the board.

The condition of the campus was appalling when I took over, and that, among other things, had discouraged community leaders and other outsiders from investing in our institution and our students. We were getting regularly nailed for code violations on our growing number of properties.

As an initial step, I brought in as a special assistant George Dandelake, who had served as my budget chief at the sheriff's office. I assigned him to assess and address our many infrastructure needs. He found a full docket of serious issues, the residue of years of financial stress and administrative inaction. Dormitories needed new air conditioners, new appliances, new water heaters, and even new windows. We had to repair and renovate bathrooms, electrical cabinets, elevators, and laundry rooms. Landscaping had to be replaced. Even the chapel needed major renovation, including the pews. George soon got a handle on all of it. He took direct oversight of budgeting, planning, and execution. The work began, and we took renewed pride in our surroundings. But we needed money for all the updates. So I visited and enlisted various friends and associates, advising them and updating them on our needs at EWC. Michael Ward, then president and chief executive officer of the major CSX railroad company, wanted to know what it would take to upgrade the campus infrastructure.

In response, he generously created the Michael Ward Matching Infrastructure Fund, donating $1 million if we could raise another $2 million within a year. And we did. Under Bishop Young's oversight, the AME Church raised and donated $1 million. We then reached out to the community, which responded positively to our fundraising efforts, bringing in approximately another $1 million. As expected, Michael kept his word after we were able to raise the $2 million within the year and donated $1 million.

Additionally, we wanted to place a sheriff's office substation on campus, with a price tag of $2.6 million. This initiative also required funding. We were able to raise close to $1 million, which was donated to us by the JSO from confiscated drug money. Then Wayne Weaver, the former owner of the Jacksonville Jaguars, worked to raise and donate $1 million. The remaining funds needed were secured through our aggressive action to secure federal, state, and local grants.

The sheriff's office substation building is now being used to educate criminology students.

Looking at the big picture, we had to identify and focus on our educational mission. We reminded ourselves that we were a Historically Black College and University located in a somewhat disadvantaged part of town and had to play to our strength. Our strength was EWC's desire and commitment to ensuring and providing quality higher education to students from underserved communities. I truly loved walking the campus, shaking hands, and chatting with the students. Some saw me as a father figure, and I was fine with that. I wanted to let them know that I cared about them.

I also had the opportunity to be a fair, objective judge when our students violated our rules. Sometimes, I had no choice but to suspend a student, but I generally left each of them with an opportunity to find a way back to EWC if he or she so desired.

When it came to underachievers—students who consistently weren't making the grade—I don't remember ever telling my people to send them home. I always said, "Find a way to keep them here." To this day, I'm not totally certain this was the wisest move that a college president could make, but, as I said, after putting people in jail for thirty-eight years, I was motivated to take steps to help others put themselves in positions where they would shine. This was the role I believed I had spent a lifetime preparing for—the most fulfilling assignment of my lifetime of service.

After less than a year as interim president, I was asked to take the job on a permanent basis. All my resistance had vanished, and I unequivocally accepted the position. Upon my inauguration on February 12, 2011, as the school's twenty-ninth permanent president, the board of trustees released this statement:

Since Glover's arrival at EWC in 2010, he has stabilized the College's financial infrastructure, developed partnerships with prominent organizations in Jacksonville to increase developmental opportunities for students, strengthened institutional morale, and led the College to the successful submission of its Fifth Year Report to the Southern Association of Colleges and Schools.

Future plans include the construction of a police substation, which will provide increased security on and around campus and classrooms for criminal justice students. This will enable them to work near and with law enforcement officers to provide real-life applications to the scenarios they study in the classroom. Also, plans are moving forward for the construction of a state-of-the-art health disparities center, which will provide health services for the community and serve as a hub for research on the common health disparities found in urban and impoverished communities.

I had come full circle at Edward Waters College. When I first arrived in 1962 on a football scholarship, I was required to do three things: play well, successfully complete my lessons, and clean that bathroom every day. Now, having sat across the hall from that bathroom, I realized that Edward Waters College had saved my life—and I think I might have helped it too.

Under the leadership of my successor, Dr. A. Zachary Faison, SACSCOC, the accreditation agency that fifteen years earlier had almost ruinously critiqued Edward Waters, approved its application to offer master's level courses and the college thereby changed its name to Edward Waters University.

From near destruction as a college to elevation as a university—I cannot imagine a more satisfying phase of a career, especially in so-called retirement.

CHAPTER 18

MY LEADERSHIP BLUEPRINT: DREAM FEARLESSLY, CARE INTENSELY, EXPECT ABUNDANTLY, AND RISK BOLDLY

You can start there, but you must leave
them better than you found them.

Given that one purpose of this book is to share lessons learned during decades of service in supervisory leadership positions, I want to take some time and space to drill deeper into what I think of as the art of leadership, which I've leveraged as the foundation for my leadership blueprint. Throughout my years of research on the topic of leadership, I have tapped into a conglomeration of leadership theories to help round out and support my core leadership values, beliefs, and perceptions. I have lectured more than 125 times on this subject and continue to do so while in retirement. I am convinced that these concepts can and, on a daily basis, do help managers—especially those in law enforcement, but also people in many other fields—become the leaders they must be to effectively supervise and nurture their staffs.

Although it's true that some people are born with greater leadership skills, the characteristics required for effective leadership end up being about the same for both categories of people. That is to say, the ability to lead is really a collection of skills, nearly all of which can be learned and improved upon, but it's a process that doesn't happen overnight.

Indeed, leadership skills are universally transferable. If you can lead police officers, you can also lead people in higher education, the corporate world, and those working in the nonprofit sector. Conditions change. You change. Social mores and expectations change. Your leadership skills must change along with them. What you want to do is learn the fundamentals of how to identify the ebbs and flows of change. Learn the techniques. Learn the dynamic. Expect excellence and do not be willing to tolerate mediocrity. Many of your people have it within them to succeed, lead, elevate, and shine, but you have to draw it out of them; you have to help them find it within themselves. That's what you should be doing and what you should require your people to do—to be better. We are here to serve the community, and we want to give the community our best effort and work.

What are the components of leadership? Some people in leadership positions think that all they must do is make sure their employees show up on time and do their work. There is far more to leadership than that. A true leader is one who has vision, courage, commitment, and the ability to inspire, motivate, and encourage people to reach their potential. This is crucial if subordinates are to achieve their personal, career, or social goals through productivity, efficiency, and effectiveness.

Too often, supervisors, managers, and leaders make decisions based on what their employees want. They may design schedules around making employees comfortable and happy, forgetting that their first responsibility is to the constituents they serve and then to the organization. That said, there's certainly nothing wrong with *considering* employee desires in the decision-making process.

A particularly important element of leadership is looking people in the eye and telling them what they need to hear, even if that is not what they *want* to hear. One of the toughest things to do as a leader is to say no. If you need to say no, say no. Don't hesitate. But do take some time to figure out how to properly, strategically, and helpfully say no.

If a person with no communication skills asks to be the organizational spokesperson, then you have to say no for the good of that person and the organization. If they tell you, "I want to be the spokesman for the organization," but you know that they have never been a great communicator, you must tell them no. Place them in a position where, with their skills and drive, they—and by extension, the organization—can achieve success and can shine. Your people must be in positions where they can be better than mediocre.

Someone may say about their coworker, "He was all right." But is that all you want your people to be? Is that all *you* want to be? No. You want to strive for people to say, "She was good." "He made a difference." "She elevated me and led me to a whole new level." That's what you're looking for. So when you begin as someone's supervisor, you should not be satisfied with OK. You can start there, but you must leave them better than you found them.

Every person who transfers from your supervision to another position should be better equipped and more skilled for having worked under your management. They want to get better, and it's your job to help them achieve that. It naturally follows, then, that leaders should feel privileged and honored to be in such a position, given that they are influential, empowered, and in a position of control over others. Like I've always challenged myself, if I have all the power and authority and I still don't make a difference, then shame on me.

When we take on a new assignment as a leader, we too often settle into the routine that was left for us. We think the people who came before us were smarter than we are. Not necessarily. The way I look at it is, they set a baseline. What we must do is take it to another, higher level. The Lord gives each of us something special. We all have something extraordinary in us, but sometimes we don't let it manifest itself. When I decided to run for sheriff, many people said, "Are you crazy, man? They don't elect Black sheriffs in Florida. Let's be honest—white people aren't going to vote for you. You're going to go out there and embarrass yourself." That's what they said. If I had listened to them, I wouldn't be sharing these words with you right now.

To distinguish yourself as a leader, take a chance. Reach higher, for yourself and for your employees, and for your employer. Are great leaders born, or is great leadership learned? The answer is: Yes. Both.

Born leaders might be blessed with charisma, confidence, decisiveness, enthusiasm, and a bit more ego than most. Learned leaders develop the ability to subordinate themselves and to act with poise, optimism, perseverance, and knowledge of the rules of engagement (in other words, making good decisions, using good judgment, and so on).

Then there's charisma, which is hard to define, but as US Supreme Court Justice Potter Stewart wrote in 1964 about obscenity: "I know it when I see it." If someone says, "She has presence," that's charisma. If someone walks into a room and you immediately think, *That's somebody*, then that's charisma. Charisma enhances credibility, an essential characteristic of leadership.

Confidence is a close cousin of charisma. Leaders must have—and must display in measured ways—confidence in themselves. Remember that anecdote I shared about going shopping for proper clothing when I was promoted to a detective? Other newbies were coming back with four or five cheap suits, but I shopped at a somewhat more prestigious store and bought two fine suits and five fine sports jackets. This gave me a sharper look, and *that* gave me more confidence. That helped me develop a narrative about myself and my ability to rise into leadership positions.

Humility is also important. That means putting other people first and remembering that it's not all about you. If you center yourself on your personal upward mobility, you'll lose credibility and de-motivate your team. You squander some of their goodwill and enthusiasm for you as a leader and set yourself up for failure. Optimism, enthusiasm, and perseverance are key ingredients of leadership. Think positively, lead with assurance, and adjust if necessary, but don't give up. I don't ever remember telling one of my bosses that I couldn't do something.

Finally, find yourself a right-hand man or woman—someone you can trust completely and rely upon without question, someone who will always tell you the way it is and not necessarily just what you want to hear. In searching for this person, look for what I call the seven Cs— candor, credibility, competence, courage, confidentiality, connectivity, and common sense.

Now, let's turn to the other side of the transaction: What do subordinates want and expect from *you*? In a nutshell, they want to know that you care about them, that they can trust you, and that you're committed to excellence. Always keep your ear to the ground, assessing how your subordinates view you. Here is a self-test that you can deploy: If one person calls you a jackass, don't worry about it. If two people call you a jackass, you should pay attention. If three people call you a jackass, you probably are a jackass. In other words, be attentive to the difference between the odd remark and an observable trend in how your subordinates experience you. The bad news is, they think you're a jackass; the good news is, now you know. You can engage in remediation.

In order to improve my relationships, I have always found it useful to make a deposit in what I call the emotional bank account. What do I mean by this? It's pretty simple, really. Work on your relationships with others and make goodwill deposits in these relationships. The currency of this account is smiles and compliments, notes of caring and sympathy when illness or death strikes close to home, or an extra day off when it's clearly needed.

One day, I may have something on my mind and unintentionally walk past an employee without a smile or acknowledgment. She could think, *What a jackass.* But what I want her to think is, *Something must be bothering him.* Ideally, she doesn't get upset because I already have some goodwill on deposit with her. On a bad day, I can make a withdrawal from that account because I made some good deposits with that employee.

I'm also big on ROI—return on investment—in my employees. You must invest in order to get that kind of return. If you don't have anything on deposit, you have nothing to withdraw. They also must know that you have their best interests at heart. That you never bad-mouth them to others. That you defend them as warranted. That if things go wrong, you will shoulder the blame to the extent possible. If you want people to follow you, they must respect you and trust you. They must also know that you are enduringly committed to excellence and that you expect that from everyone under your command. Inevitably, you will have people who come to work every day with the singular goal of punching the time clock to make sure they get paid and...that's about it. Have they made a difference? Are they productive, creative, innovative, looking for ways to take it to the next level? Probably not, unless you've created the expectation and environment with no tolerance of mediocrity. If they see that you're willing to tolerate low performance or, worse, misconduct, they will think they can get away with it in the future.

When I served as director of police services, a white training officer came to me and complained that African American women were not able to shoot well enough to pass the state-required minimum skill level for law enforcement officers. He was very clear about this—his criticism applied solely to female African American police cadets. I acknowledged his concern, and then I told him that I was willing to reassign him.

"Wait," he said. "I don't want to be reassigned."

I said, "Well, I need someone to help them qualify."

This immediately achieved a sea change in his attitude. He said he would put in extra work on weekends to support them, and I never again heard about that supposed issue. I found it interesting that he came up with a solution right there on the spot, in my office, when I said I would need to reassign him if he was unwilling to commit to excellence.

To gain your subordinates' confidence, always be honest and candid. Be quick to compliment and slow to criticize. And when you must criticize or act, make sure you are being constructive and decisive—and humane.

Case in point: One day, a female African American officer came to my office with a complaint about "being targeted" by a superior's allegedly unfair criticism of her job performance. "He's trying to fire me," she said. I told her, as gently as possible, that he was doing what I had ordered him to do. Visibly shaken, she hastily left my office. The backstory is that, even as a recruit, she was having difficulty making the grade. I ended up sanctioning her hiring, but complaints about her performance kept rolling in. We tried to salvage the situation for at least two years, but it became clear that she was in the wrong line of work. In the end, we documented the situation fully and we were able to fire her.

My commitment was to the citizens of Jacksonville, race notwithstanding. Still, I had a responsibility to her. By removing her from the force, I may have saved her life and the lives of others. Issues such as these come with the territory. They are to be expected and handled. At times, you will need to be confrontational, though not necessarily adversarial. To keep these occasions to a minimum, be sure to consult with subordinates before formal evaluations and between evaluation periods. Try to eliminate points of contention before they reach crisis levels. Among the questions you might ask: Do you think you're achieving the organization's goals? Are you achieving your own personal goals? How can I help serve as a better resource for you?

When tempted to criticize an employee, ask yourself, *Why am I being critical? Is this objective, and is it justified?* Never criticize someone to hurt them. Always give the person a way to salvage their pride. In addition, to further win confidence, always keep subordinates informed of what's going on, delegate authority, avoid criticizing your superiors (who also are your subordinates' superiors), keep your promises to your people, help them do their jobs, and support their valid interests. You also must be aware that there are costs to being a leader. You will make sacrifices in time and effort. You may have to tolerate rejection and endure criticism. You will experience loneliness and pressure, and mental and physical fatigue. And remember that sometimes, you're going to be wrong.

Effective leaders aren't petty, aren't too proud to apologize when called for, don't hold grudges, find a way to get beyond anger, and even smile when appropriate. If you have to say you're the boss, you've lost. You're not doing it right.

CHAPTER 19

FINAL THOUGHTS: ENDING THE DIVISION, PARTISANSHIP, AND HATE

**A life is more than a career.
Here's how we do better.**

I quoted MLK before, and I will do it again: "The arc of the moral universe is long, but it bends toward justice." To be a Black man breaking vocational barriers in the Deep South is to live with a lot of vitriol at times. The din of hatred becomes familiar background noise. But I have lived long enough to know that a life well lived is a potent testimony. People who positioned themselves as my enemies have been convicted of their hatred, not because I took the time to correct them but because my life's work bears out my love for the people of Jacksonville.

One day, just after I delivered a speech as sheriff, a white man lingered in the general area as I spent about thirty minutes chatting with various attendees. Finally, he slowly approached me. I wondered what it was about. As we faced each other, he looked me in the eye and said, "I want to apologize. I was part of Ax Handle Saturday. I was there." He left the impression that he was part of the group that had surrounded and tormented me that day. Now he was at the point of tears, and his apology clearly was sincere.

On another occasion, after I was out of the sheriff's office and was working with the universities, another white man came in and sat through a presentation I was making. He never said a word, even during some breaks in the action. He just sat there and stared at me in something of a defiant manner. At the end of the session, he walked up to me in what seemed like a potentially aggressive way. He said, "You know me?" I said, "Not really, though you do look familiar." He said that he had been one of my detectives. "When you became sheriff, I left. I quit. I just did not want you to be my sheriff. But I came here to tell you that I'm sorry, and I'm hoping that you'll accept my apology. The thing that makes me feel so awful is that I was also part of a group of officers who were doing everything they could do to embarrass you. I could have stopped the whole group if only I had said stop, and I didn't. I apologize for that as well. I am so embarrassed and so sorry about that. Please forgive me." His departing words were, "If I can do anything to help you, please let me know." I will never forget the emphasis that he put on *anything*.

I paused and then said: "If this is any consolation, it takes a lot of courage to say what you just said, and I accept your apology." He also was on the verge of tears.

On a third occasion, I went to an event accompanied by my administrative assistant, who was white. I was scheduled to serve as one of the session's main speakers. A Black group sponsored the event, and someone there told me that my assistant could not go in with me. "We don't let white people in the meetings, and that's our policy," they said.

Oh, lovely. Reverse discrimination. This was an easy one. "If she doesn't go in," I said, "I don't go in." We didn't go in.

So here's the point, which I imagine you've already discerned: People can change. Things can change. But we have to dig deep and take a stand. We must reach out. We must be open with one another, honest about our mistakes, and genuine in our desire to improve. This applies to our personal relationships and most certainly applies to the fix in which our nation finds itself. This rancid, downward spiral of partisanship, discord, greed, and selfishness, this denial of science and fact-based reality, must be reversed.

We're almost at the point in our nation and in much of Western civilization where we are jettisoning our democracies in order for fear-based ideologies to prevail. What's good for the citizenry, for our children and grandchildren, is less the issue than the danger of prevailing ideologies that often are based on nothing short of ignorance.

As I reflect on the events of January 6, 2021, when thousands of armed insurrectionists, inspired by and cheered on by a defeated presidential candidate, stormed Congress, attempted to overturn the election and had to be physically repelled, I am sickened. And then, in the wake of all that, legislatures in state after state launched assaults on voting rights, and some tried to legislate ways to reverse the legitimate outcomes of elections. Voting rights and the purity of elections, the very lifeblood of our democracy and the causes for which so many African Americans and others gave their lives, are now threatened.

President Joe Biden put it aptly during a July 13, 2021, speech in Philadelphia, the birthplace of our democracy:

In America, if you lose, you accept the results. You follow the Constitution. You try again. You don't call facts fake and then try to

bring down the American experiment just because you're unhappy.
That's not statesmanship. That's not statesmanship; that's selfishness.
That's not democracy; it's the denial of the right to vote. It suppresses.
It subjugates .... Have you no shame.

At the same time, extremists in political office and in dark corners of the media, uninformed by science, empathy, and good sense, did their best to discourage Americans from getting vaccinated against a pandemic that still was killing hundreds of thousands of Americans and millions of others around the world. It is beyond belief. It is toxic. It is profoundly un-American. And now, as I look back and I look forward, I am appalled and ... confused.

How can this *still* be America?

When I won my first campaign for sheriff, State Representative Willye Clayton Dennis, former president of Jacksonville's NAACP, told the *Palm Beach Post*, "We are no longer that little country town that people will pass by on their way to other places in Florida. This is a plus this city needed."

And it was. Other minorities soon reached the top tiers of the sheriff's department, and a Black man—Alvin Brown—was elected mayor of Jacksonville just eight years after I lost my bid for that office.

We have come a long way from Ax Handle Saturday, when a seventeen-year-old future Black sheriff was terrorized and chased out of downtown Jacksonville by a mob of Ku Klux Klansmen. And I am convinced that Jacksonville can now be an example for many cities in the Deep South—and maybe even for the rest of the country—for the significant advancements we have made in race relations, inclusion, and tolerance.

Since my election in 1995, the citizens of Jacksonville have been electing African Americans to significant leadership positions in the city. In addition to having had an African American sheriff and mayor,

Jacksonville currently has seven African American members on the nineteen-member city council, which includes an African American president and vice president of the city council. Moreover, the CEOs of the Jacksonville Port Authority, the Jacksonville Transportation Authority, and the former CEO of the Downtown Development Authority, who is now heading up economic development in the Jacksonville Chamber of Commerce, are African Americans. We have had an African American CEO at the Jacksonville Aviation Authority, and our current superintendent of schools is African American.

I have dedicated my life to striving for justice, public service, and giving back to my community. With the help of many good people, I pulled myself up from difficult circumstances on Minnie Street and found a place where I could shine. Now my hope is to help others land in places where they will shine and where together we can try to overcome—and bring our nation back from the precipice of injustice.

We are better than this. Let's prove it to our children and grandchildren.

SHERIFF NATHANIEL GLOVER'S ACCOMPLISHMENTS

1. Implemented a community policing concept. In 1996, department-wide training and orientation on the philosophy of community policing and the COPS Unit were initiated and implemented through in-service training. Community policing was taught to all recruits while in the training academy.

2. Shortly after his election, restructured the sheriff's office, which eliminated three deputy directors and two division chiefs and added one director of corrections. In addition, sixteen existing positions were reclassified to assistant division chiefs, requiring no increase in the number of supervisors. This reorganization resulted in a bottom-line savings of $200,000 a year. Replaced the police rank of captain with the rank of assistant chief. In addition, an examination of the agency was made to determine whether individual jobs were needed, and if so, were they being performed by the appropriate classification. Initially, sixteen police officers were moved from desk jobs to street duty, and additional officers were moved as civilians were hired to replace them.

3. Organized a Citizens Academy, whereby citizens signed up for a ten-week course (one night a week), which provided them with insight into the work that is done by the sheriff's office.

4. Placed police officers' names on their marked vehicles.

5. Placed substations all around the city, mostly in shopping centers, for convenient access to police officers and services for citizens. The substations provide mostly nonemergency services such as obtaining police reports, meeting with the zone commanders, and hosting ShAdCo meetings. Officers attend daily roll calls at the substation at the beginning of their shifts, thereby increasing police presence in their community.

6. Added fifty-one community Stop Stations, which were provided by businesses and community organizations. This provided a beat officer with the ability to access those conveniences while facilitating their report writing and other services.

7. Established Sheriff's Advisory Councils (ShAdCo) in every sector of the city. Citizens meet with zone commanders on a periodic basis and accompanied the sheriff on his walks in each subsector. The ShAdCos are the primary element of a two-way communications network between citizens and police.

8. Raised the educational requirement for police recruits from high school diploma to college degree. The Fourth Judicial Circuit Duval County Grand Jury investigated officer misbehavior and their presentment returned a number of questions to be answered. Sheriff Glover assembled a group of community leaders to provide recommendations for improvement. One of their recommendations was to require police recruits to have a college degree. This allowed JSO to hire a better educated and more rounded officer with studies in the social sciences with the goal of being more sensitive to diversity.

9. Personally conducted community walks in every subsector every year in office for a total of 408 (fifty-one every year).

10. Discontinued the use of the infamous choke hold in the JSO.

11. Limited the number of secondary employment hours an officer could work on days he/she had official duty requirements.

12. Required annual physical agility tests for incumbent officers.

13. Implemented the chain gang crew to control, modify, or improve the attitude of the most disruptive inmates within the system. Performed clean-up duties within the community such as for the departments of Streets and Highways and Parks and Recreation.

14. Purchased the Mobile Community Policing Vehicle, providing high visibility and mobility, thereby increasing police presence and interaction with citizens in the neighborhoods.

15. Replaced the aging Computer Aided Dispatch (CAD) system in use for seventeen years. Provided a nearly real time source of management information used to more effectively position the officers in the field and allow supervisors to more quickly spot trends, and at the same time expanded to six patrol zones and a sector system of policing.

16. Upgraded the Mobile Data Terminal (MDT) system and installed laptop computers as replacements for the less capable terminals in vehicles and provided officers with access to state-wide criminal justice information.

17. Upgraded the Automated Fingerprint Identification System (AFIS), putting the Jacksonville Sheriff's Office in the forefront of automated fingerprint technology, including both predetection and crime scene analysis.

18. Implemented the Victim Information Notification Everyday (VINE) system within the Jails Division. This system automatically notified victims of the crimes of stalking, domestic violence,

and sexual battery and notified families of murder victims when the perpetrator was released or transferred from the Department of Corrections. This notification enabled victims to maintain a heightened sense of security and facilitated communication with the office of the sheriff on a continuing basis concerning the status of the criminal responsible for their victimization.

19. Established a Drug Abatement Response Team (D.A.R.T.), comprised of personnel from the sheriff's office, the Code Enforcement Division, the Public Works Department, the mayor's office, and other local and state agencies, formed in 1996. This team targeted problems associated with narcotics, prostitution, and specific violations of municipal ordinances and state laws. Their goal was to enforce municipal housing and fire code violations and to close down structures identified as drug houses.

20. In October 1996, received a grant from the US Department of Justice to allow JSO to purchase nine hundred laptop computers with plug-in Cellular Digital Packet Data (CDPD) modems, which utilized commercial cellular infrastructure. This allowed JSO to totally change the mechanics of writing, reviewing, and turning in police reports so that each officer realized a time savings of one hour per eight-hour shift. This savings in time was devoted to community policing.

21. Built an ultramodern Police Athletic League building in the Arlington area of Jacksonville.

22. Built a new police academy at the Florida State College at Jacksonville North Campus on Capper Road. Fifty percent of the funds came from the state and 50 percent from the city. The facility was a state-of-the-art training academy for our region.

23. President Bill Clinton made a special trip to support the region's community policing philosophy and walked a community policing route and spoke to residents in the neighborhood. President Clinton credited his Community Oriented Policing Strategies crime program with enabling Jacksonville to lower its crime rate by hiring new officers and placing them in close, regular contact with neighborhood residents.

24. Implemented viodeotaping suspect interviews in the Detective Division.

25. Implemented "the rule of three," which gave the sheriff the discretion of promoting from the top three eligible persons on a promotions list instead of the restriction of only promoting from the top.

26. In February 1997 achieved the much-heralded level of the Law Enforcement Triple Crown Award recognition, which entailed national accreditation in law enforcement, corrections, and corrections health services. At that time, the Jacksonville Sheriff's Office was one of only twelve agencies in the nation that had received this recognition.

27. Established a courtroom sworn bailiff position, which utilized retired police officers. This allowed the agency to return approximately twenty sworn officer positions to patrol duty.

28. Created the Bicycle Unit to more effectively implement the community policing concept.

29. Designed and constructed a state-of-the-art equestrian facility in the LaVilla neighborhood. This allowed Mounted Unit officers to patrol more with less time spent transporting horses and equipment to and from the Montgomery Correctional Center.

30. Created the Florida Police Corps. This six-month police corps residential training program used federal grant monies to

provide new officers with additional instruction in critical areas, such as community policing and diversity training.

31. Instituted the Summer Youth Intervention Program, which targeted youth between the ages of twelve and seventeen who were considered at risk for becoming involved in criminal activity or who had been mandated by the judicial system. In this program, the youth were led by police officers through structured activities in the classroom, on athletic fields, and at military or civilian educational sites. Activities were designed to develop positive attitudes and life skills. Emphasis was placed upon social skills, respect for others, self-esteem, conflict resolution, self-discipline, team building, and leadership.

32. Created the Integrity Unit to conduct random and targeted integrity checks on sheriff's office employees.

33. Initiated the weekly cable television show *Signal 94*.

34. Along with incarcerated inmates, personally conducted neighborhood cleanups in communities where debris, clutter, and other unappealing trash were present. The trash had caused inhabitants of those communities to lose pride, which was a disincentive to helping law enforcement address the crime and other neighborhood challenges. We also had the help and assistance of other city service departments.

ACKNOWLEDGMENTS

Sometimes I feel like I am one of the most blessed people in the world. Without being accused of exaggeration, I survived two life-threatening events before the age of eighteen—one could characterize these as certain death episodes. As a toddler, I contracted double pneumonia. The doctors didn't believe I'd make it and instructed my mother to "just make me as comfortable as possible." Yet God's divine intervention was at hand. As a teenager, I was chased by Ku Klux Klansmen with axe handles, eager to cut my life short. Yet again, God's divine intervention was at hand.

So with two significant incidents, I opine that I stand here today under the banner of an overseer that is divine in nature. And that overseer protected me and placed people in my path who would counsel, direct, support, and help me achieve any ambitious life goals. Whatever my faith allowed me to visualize, God orchestrated a village around me to see my vision through.

I must first acknowledge my mother and father. Both were true examples of how to live a life that caused people to see your shining light. They were passionate and committed to their Christian faith and demonstrated that through their service to God and the church. My mother was a *shouting believer*—a demonstration of spiritual happiness. I never heard them talk negatively about people or act indifferently toward anyone, which created the blueprint for my life. My parents instilled in me a work ethic that accompanied me throughout my life. That work ethic often caught the attention of my employers, other leaders, and peers. It has had tremendous redeeming value.

I certainly cannot go any further without acknowledging my family, particularly my wife, who has been stellar in her support for everything I was destined to do. She has been nothing but encouraging, motivating, and inspiring and has always believed that I could do anything I set my mind to. She never complained about my long work hours or my sometimes-extended periods away from home. Instead, she was my rock, light, peace, comfort, and helpmate whom God ordained especially for me.

Marvin Young became my friend and was a model of impeccable interpersonal skills. His foresight into my potential to be an effective police officer propelled him to encourage me to continue to pursue this goal. He listened to my story, understood my desire, and took the bold step of asking the mayor to intervene in my police officer application process after it was presumed that nothing would become of it. I understand the audaciousness of his action and its significance in kicking off my career. I want to acknowledge him, and in case I haven't expressed it enough, thank him for being a part of the first step of my law enforcement journey. Sleep in peace, my friend.

This brings me to Mayor Lou Ritter, who hearkened his ear and empathy to the call for my law enforcement pursuit. While some justified shelving my application because of my so-called arrest record, he intervened with less than a subtle message that lit fires under the feet of those in charge of deciding the fate of my future opportunity and impacted the trajectory of my life. Thank you, Mayor Ritter. 'Til we meet again.

To the person who first laid on my heart and mind the possibility of running for sheriff in Jacksonville, Florida, Reverend John Newman, pastor of Mount Calvary Baptist Church in Jacksonville. Reverend Newman is a forward-thinking man who advocated for the advancement of Black leaders in political positions. He had his hand in the efforts to elect the first Black mayor in Philadelphia, Pennsylvania. His fingerprints are all over planting the seed that blossomed into my run for sheriff. His faithfulness and zeal for the limitless possibilities that Black people could and should hold office should be an inspiration to all.

Steve and Gary Pajcic are my two philanthropic-minded brothers. Thank you for agreeing to run and manage my historic campaign for sheriff. Your selflessness and commitment to this cause is something I'll never forget. When others were about the budget, you decided to run my campaign for free. Your belief in me was sincere and encouraging. I do not doubt that your expertise, impeccable organizational skills, and knowledge of politics resulted in the victory. I was and still am honored to know these two men who have been truly inspirational in their philanthropic endeavors. Because of you, I was encouraged to pursue my own impactful philanthropic initiatives. I thank God for your giving hearts and that He aligned me with friends who became like brothers. Gary, I miss you, and may you rest in peace. Steve, thank you, and allow me to give you your flowers while you're here.

And finally, I'd like to acknowledge all the people who helped make the publication of *Striving for Justice* possible: Walt Bussell, Wanyonyi Kendrick, Robert Monsky, Mike Freed, Jonathan Merkh, Justin Batt, Lauren Ward, Kenneth B. Morris, Jr., Kia Harris, Sharifa Stevens, Billie Brownell, Martin Merzer, Charlene Shirk, and Mel Parker.

REFERENCE NOTES

Preface

In 1960, Pete Seeger, Zilphia Horton, Guy Carawan, and Frank Hamilton copyrighted the song as a "derivative work." The music publishers the Richmond Organization, or TRO, and Ludlow Music own the copyright to the anthem. https://www.theatlantic.com/entertainment/archive/2016/04/we-shall-overcome-lawsuit/478068/#CX1 per *The Hollywood Reporter*, https://www.hollywoodreporter.com/business/business-news/song-publisher-agrees-we-overcome-public-domain-legal-settlement-1078906/

Introduction

"Leading Causes of Death–Males–Non-Hispanic Black–United States, 2018," Office of Health Equity at the CDC, last reviewed March 2, 2022, https://www.cdc.gov/minorityhealth/lcod/men/2018/nonhispanic-black/index.htm;

"Leading Causes of Death–Females–-Non-Hispanic Black–United States, 2018," Women's Health at the CDC, last reviewed March 3, 2022, https://www.cdc.gov/women/lcod/2018/nonhispanic-black/index.htm.

Brita Belli, "Racial Disparity in Police Shootings Unchanged Over 5 Years," *Yale News*, October 27, 2020, https://news.yale.edu/2020/10/27/racial-disparity-police-shootings-unchanged-over-5-years https://www.jacksonville.com/story/news/2021/05/25/history-madeblack-jacksonville-city-council-members-win-twotop-spots/7427170002/

David Bauerlein, "Newby Will Be Jacksonville's Third Black Council President and Will Do It as a Republican," *The Florida-Times Union*, May 25, 2021, https://www.jacksonville.com/story/news/education/2021/06/01/duval-school-board-votes-to-change-6-confederate-tiedschools-includinglee/7493301002/

Emily Bloch, "Duval School Board Votes to Rename 6 Confederate-Tied Schools,

Including Lee," *The Florida TImes-Union*, June 1, 2021, https://www.jacksonville.com/story/news/education/2021/06/01/duval-school-board-votes-to-change-6-confederate-tied-schools-including-lee/7493301002/

Chapter 1

Kenney, Patricia Drozd, "LaVilla, Florida, 1866-1887: Reconstruction dreams and the formation of a black community" (1990). UNF Graduate Theses and Dissertations. 699. https://digitalcommons.unf.edu/etd/699.

Chris Hand, "For Jake & Janet, Let's Fulfill Consolidation's Promise," The Jaxson, May 21, 2020, https://www.thejaxsonmag.com/article/for-jake-janet-lets-fulfill-consolidations-promise/.

Scott H. Podolsky, "The Changing Fate of Pneumonia as a Public Health Concern in 20th-Century America and Beyond," *American Journal of Public Health* 95, no. 12 (December 2005): 2144–2154, https://doi.org/10.2105/AJPH.2004.048397.

E.A. Torriero, "Barriers Fall with Election," *South Florida Sun-Sentinel*, June 18, 1995, https://www.sun-sentinel.com/news/fl-xpm-1995-06-18-9506180039-story.

Chapter 3

Florida Times-Union Editorial Board, "Editorial Board: An Apology for Failing to Adequately Cover Ax Handle Saturday," *The Florida-Times Union*, August 21, 2020, https://www.jacksonville.com/story/opinion/editorials/2020/08/21/a-1/5598641002/.

Chapter 4

Don Calloway, "Don't Let the Less Famous HBCUs Get Left Behind," *Washington Post*, July 12, 2021, https://www.washingtonpost.com/opinions/2021/07/12/its-great-timebe-howard-what-about-struggling-hbcus/.

Chapter 5

"Jacksonville Police Department: Jacksonville's African-American Police Officers," The Jacksonville Historical Society, accessed April 12, 2023, https://www.jaxhistory.org/portfolio-items/jacksonville-police-department-jacksonvilles-african-american-police-officers/.

E. Fuller Torrey, "Ronald Reagan's Shameful Legacy: Violence, the Homeless, Mental Illness," *Salon*, September 29, 2013, https://www.salon.com/2013/09/29/ronald_reagans_shameful_legacy_violence_the_homeless_mental_illness/.

Wikipedia, s.v. "Baker Act," last modified March 23, 2023, 23:47, https://en.wikipedia.org/wiki/Florida_Mental_Health_Act.

Chapter 6

"Jacksonville Police Department: Jacksonville's African-American Police Officers," The Jacksonville Historical Society, accessed April 12, 2023, https://www.jaxhistory. org/portfolio-items/jacksonville-police-department-jacksonvilles-african-american-police-officers/.

Chapter 7

"Charge He Hijacked Bus, for Something to Do," *Daily News*, April 4, 1977, https:// www.newspapers.com/image/482433141/.

Chapter 9

Interview with Steve Pajcic, March 24, 2021.

Chapter 10

Interview with Steve Pajcic, March 24, 2021.
Interview with Steve Pajcic, March 24, 2021.
https://tour.unf.edu/#!BLD_2013042335551

Chapter 11

"The African American Odyssey: A Quest for Full Citizenship," Library of Congress, accessed April 13, 2023, https://www.loc.gov/exhibits/african-american-odyssey/ reconstruction.
"Lynching in America," PBS, accessed April 13, 2023, https://www.pbs.org/wgbh/ americanexperience/features/emmett-lynching-america/.
Jeffrey A. Butts and Jeremy Travis, "The Rise and Fall of American Youth Violence: 1980 to 2000," Urban Institute, 2002, https://www.urban.org/sites/default/files/ publication/60381/410437-The-Rise-and-Fall-of-American-Youth-Violence.PDF.

Chapter 12

Frances Robles, "Abducted at Birth and Found 18 Years Later, Woman Tries On New Identity," *New York Times*, January 18, 2017, https://www.nytimes.com/ 2017/01/18/us/alexis-anigo-kamiyah-mobley-kidnapping.html.

Chapter 13

Tony Plohetski, "Forceful Talk: In Secretly Taped Meeting, Austin Top Cop Art Acevedo Vents over High-Profile Minority Policing Failures," *Austin American-Statesman*, October 20, 2016, http://specials.mystatesman.com/art-acevedo-forceful-talk/.

Tim Arango, "Derek Chauvin Is Sentenced to 22 and a Half Years for Murder of George Floyd," *New York Times*, June 25, 2021, https://www.nytimes.com/2021/06/25/us/derek-chauvin-22-and-a-half-years-george-floyd.html.

Joey Flechas and Charles Rabin, "Houston Police Chief Brings Bravado to Miami PD: 'We Will Not Tolerate Mediocrity,'" *Miami Herald*, March 15, 2021, https://www.miamiherald.com/news/local/community/miami-dade/article249938688.html.

Cedric L. Alexander, "Which Side Are You On? The Question Every Police Officer Must Answer," *Washington Post*, March 16, 2021, https://www.washingtonpost.com/opinions/2021/03/16/police-officer-values-heart/.

"LAPD Investigating Report of George Floyd Photo Circulating with Caption 'You Take My Breath Away,'" February 13, 2021, *LA Times*, https://www.latimes.com/california/story/2021-02-13/lapd-employee-posts-photo-of-george-floyd-with-caption-you-take-my-breath-away.

Maureen Dowd, "The Ascension of Bernie Sanders," *New York Times*, July 10, 2021, https://www.nytimes.com/2021/07/10/opinion/bernie-sanders-interview-maureen-dowd.html.

"Highest to Lowest—Prison Population Total," World Prison Brief, accessed April 13, 2023, https://www.prisonstudies.org/highest-to-lowest/prison-population-total?-field_region_taxonomy_tid=All.

Emma Caplan, "Incarceration Rates by State," World Atlas, September 30, 2020, https://www.worldatlas.com/articles/highest-incarceration-rates-by-state.html.

Paula McMahon, "14-Year-Old Sentenced to Life in Prison Without Parole," *Sun-Sentinel*, March 9, 2001, https://www.sun-sentinel.com/local/broward/sfl-tatesentencing-story.html.

"Lionel Tate Pleads Guilty in Robbery," CBS News, December 19, 2005, https://www.cbsnews.com/news/lionel-tate-pleads-guilty-in-robbery/.

https://cdn.ymaws.com/counciloncj.org/resource/collection/4683B90A-08CF-493F-89EDA0D7C4BF7551/Trends_in_Correctional_Control_-_FINAL.pdf.

Nathaniel Glover, "Glover Calls for Reform of the Criminal Justice System," *Florida Times-Union*, July 19, 2020, https://www.jacksonville.com/story/opinion/columns/2020/07/19/glover-calls-for-reform-of-criminal-justicesystem/41760531/.

Glover, "Glover Calls for Reform."

Chapter 14

"Judge Demographics and Statistics In The US," Zippia, updated September 9, 2022, https://www.zippia.com/judge-jobs/demographics/; "Criminalization and Racial Disparities," Vera, accessed April 13, 2023, https://www.vera.org/ending-mass-incarceration/criminalization-racial-disparities.

Nathaniel Glover, "Glover Calls for Reform of the Criminal Justice System," *Florida Times-Union*, July 19, 2020, https://www.jacksonville.com/story/opinion/columns/2020/07/19/glover-calls-for-reform-of-criminal-justicesystem/41760531/.

"Police Forces Have Long Tried to Weed Out Extremists in the Ranks. Then Came the Capitol Riot," *New York Times*, February 16, 2021, https://www.nytimes.com/2021/02/16/us/police-extremists-capitol-riot.html.

Ben Grunwald and John Rappaport, "The Wandering Officer," *Yale Law Journal*, 2020, https://www.yalelawjournal.org/pdf/GrunwaldRappaportArticle_s6branzy.pdf.

Kim Barker, Michael H. Keller, and Steve Eder, "How Cities Lost Control of Police Discipline," *New York Times*, December 22, 2020, https://www.nytimes.com/2020/12/22/us/police-misconduct-discipline.html.

"A Special Unit to Prosecute Police Killings Has No Convictions," *New York Times*, February 26, 2021, https://www.nytimes.com/2021/02/26/nyregion/new-york-police-accountability.html.

"Florida Gov. DeSantis Signs Police Reform Legislation Requiring Use-of-Force Policies," *Naples Daily News*, June 30,2021, https://www.naplesnews.com/story/news/2021/06/30/florida-gov-desantis-signs-police-reform-legislation-use-of-forcepolicies/7795212002/.

Hassan Kanu, "U.S. Supreme Court's 'Miranda' Decision Further Guts 150-Year-Old Civil Rights Law," Reuters, June 27, 2022, https://www.reuters.com/legal/government/us-supreme-courts-mirandadecision-further-guts-150-year-old-civil-rights-law-2022-06-27/.

Chapter 15

"Those Who Would Be Mayor," News4JAX, transcript, March 11, 2003, https://www.news4jax.com/news/2003/03/11/those-who-would-be-may-or/.

"2003 Duval County First Election: 4/15/2003," Duval Elections, last updated June 21, 2006, https://www.duvalelections.com/portals/duval/archive/ERSummary.aspx38.htm.

"Racist Graffiti Mars Mayor's Race," 7KPLC News, May 14, 2003, https://www.kplctv.com/story/1277938/racist-graffiti-mars-mayors-race/.

"2003 General Election: 5/13/2003," Duval Elections, last updated June 20, 2006, https://www.duvalelections.com/portals/duval/archive/ERSummary.aspx36.htm.

Chapter 16

Brian Resnick, "Chart: One Year of Prison Costs More Than One Year at Princeton," *The Atlantic*, November 1, 2011, https://www.theatlantic.com/national/archive/2011/11/chart-one-year-ofprison-costs-more-than-one-year-atprinceton/247629/.

Anthony P. Carnevale, Stephen J. Rose, and Ban Cheah, "The College Payoff: Education, Occupations, Lifetime Earnings," Georgetown University, 2011, https://cew.georgetown.edu/cew-reports/the-college-payoff/.

Editorial Board, "Editorial: The good of The Promise Extends Far Beyond Kalamazoo," MLive, October 12, 2010, https://www.mlive.com/opinion/kalamazoo/2010/10/editorial_the_good_of_the_prom.html.

Ouida Y. Powe, "The Jacksonville Commitment Scholars Program: Graduates' Perceptions of Supports and Challenges," University of North Florida, 2015, https://digitalcommons.unf.edu/cgi/viewcontent.cgi?article=1607&context=etd.

"The Jacksonville Commitment Scholarship," University of North Florida, accessed April 13, 2023, https://www.unf.edu/scholarships/jaxcommitment.html.

https://www.jacksonville.com/article/20110505/NEWS/801252217

Chapter 17

57 Interview with Bishop A.J. Richardson, Eleventh Episcopal District, African Methodist Episcopal Church, June 8, 2021.

"Remarks by President Biden on Protecting the Sacred, Constitutional Right to Vote," White House transcript, July 13, 2021, https://www.whitehouse.gov/briefing-room/speeches-remarks/2021/07/13/remarks-by-president-biden-onprotecting-the-sacred-constitutional-right-to-vote/.